M000118888

How to Retire *from* Being a Landlord

RICHARD D. GANN, JD
JASON L. McMURTRY, MBA

How to Retire from Being a Landlord
Copyright © 2020 Richard D. Gann and Jason L. McMurtry.

All rights reserved. No part of this publication may be reproduced, stored in a retrieval system, or transmitted, in any form or by any means, electronic, mechanical, photocopying, recording or otherwise, without the prior permission of the publishers.

The authors assert the moral right to be identified as the authors of this work.

First Edition, 2020

Kindle Direct Publishing

ISBN: 978-0-578-63085-4

1031 Capital Solutions
Portland, OR

Visit *1031CapitalSolutions.com* for bulk book purchases.

Book design by Bethany Guajardo using Adobe® InDesign.®
Set in Adobe Caslon Pro by Adobe® for the body text and Gotham for the chapter titles and headers • TeamBeth.com

Foreword

by Richard D. Gann and Jason L. McMurtry

Individual investors like you own two-thirds of all rental properties in the United States.* This book is for you.

Jason and I have spent our entire careers helping clients—mostly seniors—improve the quality of their lives through better planning and investing. We started together as a young financial planner and attorney, doing seminars in libraries and coffee shops. Whether someone needed help with a property-tax assessment or avoiding probate or protecting their home in the event of catastrophic health-care costs, people and their real estate were at the core of our services from the beginning.

Over time and with more experience, both Jason and I gained exposure to more complex cases. We helped families and businesses deal with ever-larger estates and greater tax-planning issues. Because real estate investing is so common across affluent households, it was inevitable that we would develop a solid knowledge base around rental properties and how they are taxed.

I worked on my first §1031 exchange as an attorney is 1998. In that transaction, my clients exchanged an interest in a grocery-anchored shopping center in Arizona for a triple-net leased Rite Aid in Indiana. Complicating matters, the deal coincided with the dissolution of a partnership in which my clients had discovered that the managing partner was skimming funds from the property. We took great care to ensure that the exchange was structured properly under IRS rules, all while litigation was looming. The transaction certainly was not a run-of-the-mill §1031 deal, but it all worked out in the end (though to this day I feel the managing partner got off too easy in the settlement).

That case piqued my interest in §1031 exchanges, which

complemented my existing practice in property and estate taxes. After a few more years of working with legal and financial clients directly, I joined Jason on the "manufacturing" side of the business. He and I spent a dozen years working for large real estate firms in Southern California, syndicating §1031 real estate programs and other public and private funds. During that phase of our careers, we gained invaluable knowledge about real estate underwriting, finance, taxation, regulation and investing. In addition to our respective graduate degrees (JD and MBA), we both have been licensed in real estate, insurance and financial planning.

Jason and I have owned multiple homes, rental properties and REITs. We have syndicated and distributed properties in over a dozen states, across sectors including multifamily, industrial, office, retail and healthcare. And now that I live in Oregon, I get to enjoy a whole new regime of taxes and regulations, almost as byzantine and costly as California's. Drawing from all of this experience, we endeavored to write this book for you, the individual landlord seeking to "retire" from owning and operating your own rental property.

This book is an overview. Each topic in these chapters could be the sole subject of a textbook. In today's short-attention-span world, we have tried to strike a balance between brevity and quality. If you come away from certain sections desiring more information, we encourage you to search Amazon for additional resources or contact us directly. Furthermore, please be mindful of the dynamic nature of regulations, especially with regard to taxation. The more political a policy area is, the more likely it is to change. Rent control, tort law and taxes are highly politicized topics; as more time passes after this book is published, readers should be increasingly careful to double-check current rules and tax tables.

Too many people are holding on to rental properties for the wrong reasons. We hope this book will help you make a more informed decision to keep, sell or possibly replace your current rental property. If we can be of further assistance, please let us know.

-*Richard D. Gann,*

Managing Partner, 1031 Capital Solutions

For those wishing to embark on a career in real estate investing, an entire industry stands ready to offer support. From training books, videos and seminars on how to purchase your first rental property, to lenders, real estate brokers, property managers, book-keeping services, industry associations and other vendors, a virtual army of service providers is available to offer help every step of the way. With the aid of this support system, many people have found real estate to be a terrific way to accumulate wealth and defer taxes during their working years—setting up for a potentially great retirement.

But there is a problem: unlike a traditional employment arrangement, a career in real estate investing does not offer a retirement plan. The same real estate investments that created so much tax-sheltered wealth can later become one of the largest sources of burden and stress, both financially and emotionally. Real estate investors may report feeling overwhelmed and handcuffed to the very property they thought would provide their financial freedom in retirement. The continuous challenge of dealing with tenants, maintenance and regulations creates the burden and years of capital-gains-tax deferral that become the handcuffs. Successful real estate investors across the country are reaching their golden years and asking, "How can I retire from my real estate"?

One answer to this question lies at the intersection of finance where real estate, securities and tax law converge—an investment strategy that has been available for many years, yet has only gained wide popularity over the past decade or so. When the IRS issued Revenue Ruling 2004-86 giving guidance on Delaware Statutory

Trusts ("DSTs") as §1031 exchange replacement properties in 2004, the popularity of this strategy exploded. In 2019—the year this book was written—investors acquired over seven billion dollars of real estate in the form of DST programs.**

Understanding the benefits, risks and limitations of using DSTs to retire from real estate requires an understanding of tax laws, including §1031 exchange rules, real estate and U.S. securities regulations. This book offers a basic education in these three areas, and addresses a variety of ancillary issues and alternative strategies to escape the burdens of real estate ownership on a tax-favored basis.

While many CPAs may have an understanding of tax law, many do not have an equally deep understanding of securities regulations or real estate issues. Likewise, a real estate broker knows real estate but may lack in tax or securities knowledge. A financial advisor surely understands basic investing and portfolio management principles, but is frequently deficient in knowledge related to real estate investing or tax law.

We hope you will find that our background and experience make us uniquely qualified to write this book and help you retire from being a landlord.

-Jason L. McMurtry,
Managing Partner, 1031 Capital Solutions

Additional notes from the authors:

- We use the symbol § in lieu of "Section". For example, §1031 refers to Section 1031 of the Internal Revenue Code.
- Unless otherwise noted, when we refer to "yield", we mean the Equity Yield Rate, as defined and explained in Chapters IIIA and IIIB. This metric factors in loan interest, while Net Operating Income (NOI) represents revenues minus expenses,

but before deducting interest, taxes and depreciation.

- We use the term "program" to refer to an investment offering in which funds are pooled from multiple people to acquire and operate a small portfolio of real estate.

- We have deviated from the strict traditional conventions for citing sources to reflect our modern Internet-based society. Where appropriate, we directly cite the web pages where information was found, or where you may find additional resources on the topic.

- The views and opinions expressed in this book are for informational purposes only as of the date of this material and are subject to change at any time. This material is not a recommendation, offer or solicitation to buy or sell any securities or engage in any particular investment strategy, and should not be considered specific legal, investment or tax advice.

- Please speak with your own tax and legal advisors for guidance regarding your particular situation. Because investor situations and objectives vary, this information is not intended to indicate suitability for any particular investor. Company names listed herein may have proprietary interests in their names and trademarks. Nothing herein shall be considered to be an endorsement, authorization or approval of the aforementioned companies, or the investment vehicles they may offer. Further, none of the aforementioned companies are affiliated with the authors or their affiliates in any manner. Hypothetical examples and scenarios used throughout this material are for illustration purposes only; individual results may vary.

*According to a 2015 report from the U.S. Census Bureau (https://www.census.gov/news-room/press-releases/2017/rental-housing.html), individual investors own 74.4% of all rental housing properties. 14.8% are owned by LPs, LLPs and LLCs, and trusts/estates own another 4.1%. On a per-unit basis, rather than a per-property basis, individuals own 47.8% of rental housing, followed by LPs/LLPs/LLCs (33.2%) and trusts/estates (3.3%). In this book, we refer to "individual landlords" to include single people, couples and families, who often create an LP or LLC to take title to their property. Assuming half of the LPs/LLPs/LLCs indicated by the Bureau fall into this group, and including trusts/estates in our definition of individual landlords (as opposed to corporations, REITs, or other institutional owners), than individual investors own 85.9% of all rental-housing *properties* and 67.7% of all rental housing *units*.
** Mountain Dell Consulting, LLC

TABLE OF CONTENTS

PART I
DECIDING TO SELL

This page intentionally left blank

CHAPTER 1

As If You Didn't Already Know:
The Drudgery of Owning Investment Real Estate

TENANTS

For individual investors who buy property for its current income, the best aspect of owning real estate is depositing rent checks.

Yet many landlords would admit that the worst part of owning real estate, at times, is dealing with the source of those checks—their tenants.

Before you can start cashing those late rent payments, you must first find the tenants to mail them. Depending on your property type, this process can range from seeking college students to small businesses. You may need to incur significant marketing expenses and pay substantial finders' fees. In some instances, even more costly than new-tenant expenditures is the value of lost time between move-ins.

Assuming your marketing program generates viable leads, filling vacancies starts with screening. Most landlords fail to thoroughly vet all candidates, as the process is both cumbersome and time-consuming. Applicants' former landlords are reluctant or refuse to discuss tenants in fear of litigation. Background checks may omit important data if you are not willing to pay for good reports. And if you subject only some people to background checks but not others, you may be subject to anti-discrimination lawsuits. In cities like Portland, Oregon, there are complex regulations for bringing on new tenants that are easy for well-meaning owners to violate.

After filtering prospective tenants through background checks, referral interviews and job verifications, landlords then must entice renters to sign a lease agreement. If you own a retail center or small office property, your new lessee may have her own broker, attorney, or both. Days or even weeks can be wasted arguing over boilerplate lease provisions because your would-be renter has a friend who just graduated from law school. Is it really worth spending a month's rent to have an attorney negotiate a simple lease? Probably not.

Unlike institutionally-managed apartment communities, individual landlords of smaller residential properties simply do not have the resources to ensure ideal renter profiles. Large apartment operators employ sophisticated search-engine optimization tools for their rental websites, rely on regional or nationwide brand recognition for referrals and use expensive software that calculates rental rates on a daily basis. For regular folks, getting "good" tenants and setting the right rent is often a matter of luck.

Once in the door, tenants' regular "wear and tear" can escalate into damage and destruction. In some cases, the cause of extensive loss may be truly accidental—an iron left on or a clogged toilet. On the other hand, real vandalism may be to blame. According to TransUnion, 21% of apartment properties have at least one renter with a criminal record.[1] If you own multiple units, you could be sheltering one or more convicts on your property.

Criminal or not, today's tenants are increasingly burdened by the cost of housing as a percentage of their disposable income. Indeed, while a 3:1 ratio of income-to-rent is supposed to be the "industry standard", an estimated 40% of renters use half their income to pay their landlords.[2] For small-business tenants, rent may be one of their highest monthly expenses.

Which is why so many tenants—millions per year—ultimately face eviction. As charitable as we may want to be, most landlords rely heavily on their property income, often to support their retirement.

Most individual owners are lenient and sympathetic toward chronically tardy rent-payers, but when one of your three tenants stops paying rent altogether, losing a third of your income is simply not acceptable.

EVICTION

Frustratingly, initiating eviction is just the beginning of a long and expensive process. Eviction-related expenses average more than $3,500 in the United States and can take several weeks or longer in states like California.[3] In that state, after a renter is in default for three days, a landlord must first serve the tenant with a Notice to Quit. The tenant's failure to comply results in an Unlawful Detainer lawsuit. Upon being served with a complaint, the tenant then has either five or 15 days to respond (depending on the form of service) with an Answer. Once the Answer is filed, the landlord's attorney may need to engage in discovery. Eventually one of the parties will request a trial date, which must be set between 10 and 20 days after the request. After the landlord obtains a judgment, she must file a Writ of Possession, which the Sheriff's Department will post on the property at least 20 days from the date of judgment. If the tenant is still squatting at this point, a Sheriff's deputy will remove him/her and replace the locks. All told, this process in the Golden State takes between 45 and 75 days![4]

Let us now suppose your condo tenant vacated the premises without eviction and with proper notice. There were no complaints from neighbors and rent usually was paid on time. You enter the front door on move-out day in a moderately pleasant mood, only to find a home that has aged 10 years in 12 months. What can you do?

Taking a step back, you were supposed to do a semi-annual inspection of this (and every) unit, with note-taking and photography. Yet many landlords neglect this chore, as it is a scheduling hassle and can be awkward if not confrontational. Unauthorized pets and tenants also come to light during site inspections—these new additions may be difficult to remove depending on local regulations. Instead of facing these issues directly, owners often choose to ignore what is happening inside their properties and hope for a minimal surprise on move-out day.

Conversely, if you discovered the damage in the course of removing a residential tenant for cause, be prepared for the possibility of two separate legal actions. In Oregon, most landlords must pursue their evictions in courts dedicated to Forcible Entry and Wrongful Detainer lawsuits, also known as "FED Court". Uninitiated plaintiffs in FED Court are often angry upon learning that FED Court does not award damages—only the landlord's right to re-possession (if granted). To seek an award for unpaid rent or reimbursement for property damage beyond normal wear and tear, landlords must follow FED Court with a separate lawsuit in Small Claims Court (or Superior Court, depending on the extent of the damages).

The natural reaction upon discovering damages is to rely on the tenant's security deposit to make the unit ready for the next move-in. But in states such as California, you may be strictly limited in your use of deposit funds to mitigate renter defacement. Worse, in 2019 Oregon passed a law that limits deposits to 1½ month's rent!* State tenant protection laws—and small-claims courts—generally favor renters and make it difficult for landlords to keep any deposit dollars, as judges often interpret "normal wear and tear" quite broadly. And if a tenant is found to have actually damaged,

---

* Up to two months' rent if the applicant has particularly bad screening results.

say, a carpet or countertop or appliance, some jurisdictions may limit the tenant's liability to only a fraction of the replacement cost, based on the "useful life" of the damaged item. Fair or not, you simply cannot use what little security deposits you may have to return your property to a rentable condition.

Here is a flow chart representing the eviction process in California:

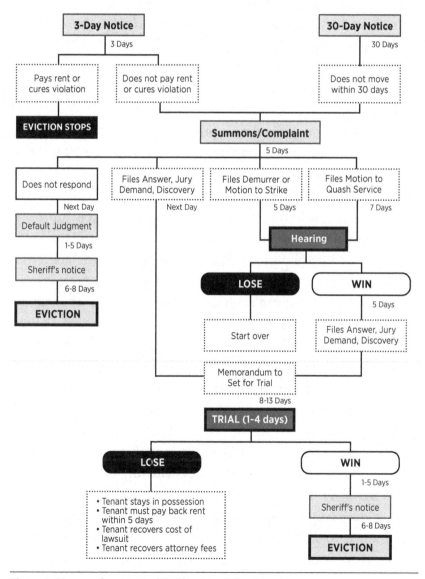

Figure 1: Diagram for a typical California eviction.[5]

RENT CONTROL

In the broadest sense, "rent control" includes statutory schemes that do one or more of the following:

- Regulate the timing or frequency of increasing tenants' rent
- Regulate/require services that landlords must provide to tenants
- Limit the grounds on which a landlord may evict tenants

Today, multiple jurisdictions have adopted some form of rent control, including cities in D.C., Maryland, New Jersey, New York and most recently, Oregon and California, which in 2019 became the first two states to enact a statewide rent-control law. Here is what Oregonian owners face today, and you could face in the future:[6]

Annual rental increases on continuing tenants capped at 7% plus inflation (new construction exempt for 15 years)

There have been times in recent years when average YOY rent increases exceeded 7%. On an aggregate basis, this law would have cost Oregon landlords millions of dollars in lost rent in those years. Rent control restrictions provide no relief to landlords during recessionary periods, while capping landlords' ability to make up for down years when conditions are more favorable.

Causes for evictions are restricted after first year of tenancy

If a new residential tenant has a 12-month lease that expires, and she continues to live in the unit on a month-to-month basis, her landlord no longer has the ability to terminate the occupancy without cause. Effectively, without meeting very specific requirements, landlords cannot get rid of tenants after they have lived in the property for a year.

Landlords are required to pay one month's rent to tenants when evicting for landlord reoccupation or renovations (with 90 days' notice)

Imagine you have been renting out your former home, currently on a month-to-month basis, to someone who has been there for two years. Your new home is destroyed in a fire, and you need to move back into your former residence. In order to reoccupy your home, you now will need to provide extended notice and give the tenants the equivalent of one month's rent for their inconvenience.

Tenants are allowed to cure violations in many instances rather than be evicted outright

The possibility of eviction is often the only factor keeping bad tenants from becoming outright nightmares. Now people can confidently violate their lease terms and remain in place by simply "curing" the problem.

A landlord who breaks the rules may be liable for three months' rent plus actual damages

In a blatant example of anti-landlord bias, this provision slaps landlords with a punitive-damage penalty that does not exist for tenants.

Even worse, certain large cities like Seattle, Oakland and Portland recently have imposed egregious new regulations and restrictions on residential landlords, including:

- prohibiting the use of criminal background checks
- limiting the use of financial background checks
- possibly requiring acceptance of previously evicted tenants
- forcing quiet periods between advertising and accepting rental applications
- mandating distribution of copious disclosures to applicants
- capping landlords' monthly income requirements (e.g., 2.5 x rent)
- preventing reimbursement from tenants when replacing older appliances
- limiting security deposits to 1.5 x month's rent

MAINTENANCE AND CAPITAL EXPENDITURES

A well-known website for landlords lists over 40 websites for helping owners with maintenance and repairs. U.S. revenues for contracted real estate maintenance services are estimated to be over $180 billion in 2019.[7] This figure underscores the depth and breadth of the property-maintenance industry, largely paid for (directly or indirectly) by landlords. Whether you do it yourself or rely on help, your responsibility to maintain your property undoubtedly requires considerable time and money.

The following section is a partial list of maintenance items with which most residential landlords must contend. Have you (or your property manager) been diligently performing these chores, regularly, for all of your units?

While these listed items may be numerous, they are not the "big ticket" items that property owners dread. The largest threats to your wallet likely will come from these types of repairs and capital expenditures:

Maintenance Checklist

- ❏ Inspect roofing for damages and leaks
- ❏ Repair or replace siding or stucco
- ❏ Seal cracks and gaps in windows and doors with caulk or weather stripping
- ❏ Clear out gutters and downspouts
- ❏ Fill cracks and gaps in driveways and sidewalks
- ❏ Fertilize and mow lawn
- ❏ Prune trees and shrubs
- ❏ Pull weeds
- ❏ Mend or replace fence
- ❏ Wash windows
- ❏ Wipe/vacuum heat registers
- ❏ Check all air vents and ducts for blockage
- ❏ Clean/replace furnace filter
- ❏ Check and clean fireplace flues
- ❏ Check water softener, replenish salt
- ❏ Clean kitchen exhaust fan filter
- ❏ Vacuum refrigerator freezer coils, clean drip trays
- ❏ Check around kitchen and bathroom cabinets and around toilets for leaks
- ❏ Unclog tub and sink drains
- ❏ Test smoke and carbon monoxide alarms, replace batteries
- ❏ Inspect electrical cords and wires
- ❏ Flush out water heater sediment
- ❏ Paint, paint, paint
- ❏ Clean, steam or replace carpets
- ❏ Oil squeaky handles and repair loose locks
- ❏ Inspect sprinkler systems
- ❏ Check basement for leaks
- ❏ Re-stain/finish decking
- ❏ Replace common-area deck furniture
- ❏ Hire pro to inspect and pump

- ❏ Clean faucets and showerheads to remove mineral deposits
- ❏ Oil garage-door opener and chain
- septic tank
- ❏ Seal tile grout

COMPLIANCE WITH TAX RULES

Later in this book, we will dedicate several pages to the concepts of depreciation and capital gains. If you are familiar with these core principles of rental-property taxation, you know that careful record keeping and receipt retention is required to prove your "cost basis" in the future.

Roof replacement

HVAC replacement

Flood damage/pipe replacement

Parking lot re-slurry

Fallen tree repair and removal

Foundation repair

Using 1099 forms with contractors and service providers is also very important. Under IRS rules, you are obligated to issue a 1099 form to most non-incorporated people who charge you at least $600 in a year. For example, if an electrician works on two of your rental properties and, over the course of a couple visits, bills you for $700, you must file a 1099 form by January 31 (as of the writing of this book). After January, there may be a late fee of $50, and after August 1 the penalty could be as high as $270.

This is especially true if you want to claim the "199A Deduction", which was added into law as of 2017. 199A provides a deduction on certain business income—including rental income—earned by many small businesses and sole proprietors (as of 2019, married couples with income below $321,400 reap the most rewards from the deduction rules, as higher-earning households have declining deductions). To claim the 199A deduction, a landlord's property must be producing a net profit.

Further, the landlord's income must be considered to be coming from a "trade or business". The IRS has issued "safe harbor" rules for what constitutes a trade or business under 199A, but many CPAs believe that these rules are difficult for mom-and-pop rental owners to meet. As a result, some individuals may have to jump through several hoops to claim the same deductions that slightly larger businesses receive more readily.

As with every topic in this book, always consult with your tax or legal professional.

MISCELLANEOUS HEADACHES

In addition to the more common issues discussed above, here is just a sampling of the random—but no less irksome—hassles or crises that many landlords can expect to experience over time:

Residential

- Noise and party complaints
- Tenant conflicts with neighbors
- Tenant conflicts with each other
- HOA compliance
- Plumbing/electrical emergencies
- Police visits and criminal activity
- Tenant deaths
- Rodents

Commercial

- Public trash and dumpsters
- Property safety/surveillance
- Security alarms
- Parking violations
- Signage and other code enforcement
- Skaters on railings
- Bigger rodents

Hiring a property-management company to handle these issues does not necessarily make them go away. Rather, you may just get calls from the manager, rather than the tenant, to have you deal with these problems.

Unless you own a property subject to a triple-net lease, you are probably also responsible for all of your property taxes and insurance. Some states have opaque taxation laws that allow state or local governments to surprise you with increased assessments and bond taxes. Navigating insurance providers can be a full-time job, an area where national operators have a distinct advantage over mom-and-pop landlords. And failing to pay either type of bill can have expensive, if not devastating, consequences. However, the greatest potential downside to owning investment real estate as an individual landlord is legal liability. We address this scary specter in the next section.

This page intentionally left blank

CHAPTER 2

A Dark Reality:
Legal Liability for Individual Landlords Has Never Been Worse

---

When you own rental real estate, you expose yourself—and your assets—to a whole new world of potential legal liability. It is possible to mitigate this risk by holding title through business entities (LLCs, corporations, irrevocable trusts, etc.) and purchasing insurance policies, though the latter can often encourage, rather than deter, litigation. Even if you can protect your personal assets, litigation itself can be highly damaging to both your wallet and psyche. As an individual owner of an investment property, you will be the target of any property-related lawsuit, regardless of whether you hold title in an LLC or have excellent insurance.

In this chapter, we remind you about three of the major categories of possible landlord exposure: fair housing laws, premises liability and mold.

FAIR HOUSING LAWS

Federal, state and local laws protect tenants from discrimination because of their race, color, national origin, religion, creed and sex/gender. Such laws also may prohibit discrimination due to the presence of children, disability, sexual orientation, gender identity, marital status and military history. The U.S. Department of Housing and Urban Development ("HUD") enforces federal fair-housing laws, while various state agencies or commissions oversee corresponding state rules. Further, some municipal jurisdictions have additional discrimination protections on their books, including discrimination against Section 8 voucher holders.

Specifically, fair housing laws prohibit the following actions:[8]

- Refusing to rent to someone or misrepresenting the availability of a rental unit because of the person's protected class.
- Discriminating in the terms and conditions of rental because of a resident's protected class. This includes creating unequal rules or regulations against a particular group of people, unequal enforcement of rental agreement rules or denying access to amenities based on a tenant's membership in a protected class.
- Publishing a notice, statement or advertisement that indicates any preference, limitation or discrimination based on a protected class. For example, advertising a preference for a Catholic tenant is discriminatory against non-Catholics.
- Not providing reasonable accommodations to a person with a disability, refusing to allow a disabled resident to make necessary modifications or failing to provide required access.
- Enforcing a neutral rule or policy that has a disproportionately adverse effect on a protected class, unless there is a valid business reason for the rule or policy, and the housing provider can show that there is no less discriminatory means of achieving the same result.
- Retaliating against a resident or applicant because he or

she has asserted fair housing rights or has been a witness in a fair housing investigation. This rule applies both to informal verbal complaints and formal discrimination cases filed with an agency. Although the original allegation may be unfounded, if a housing provider takes retaliatory action, a tenant likely can support a retaliation complaint. In other words, a landlord must simply take it on the chin when a tenant files a claim.

Fair housing laws also protect applicants and tenants associated with people in protected groups. This includes scenarios where a landlord allegedly discriminates because the prospective resident has friends or relatives in any of the protected categories.

Unquestionably, there can be no tolerance for an owner who purposefully seeks to discriminate in any of the ways described above. However, well-intending landlords can easily trip over these rules, which are designed to make it easy for tenants to make and pursue their claims.

Regardless of the merits, if HUD or an equivalent state agency brings a charge, you will need to attend several hearings and defend the claim before a HUD or other administrative law judge (which way do you suppose this official is leaning?). Alternatively, the U.S. Department of Justice ("DOJ") may pursue a case against you on behalf of the claimant. You most likely will need to hire an attorney.

In either instance, the complainant may be awarded compensatory damages that include:[9]
- Out-of-pocket expenses while finding alternative housing
- Rent fees associated with alternative housing
- Legal fees to process the claim
- Non-economic damages (e.g., for mental anguish)

On the following page are the 2018 inflation-adjusted civil penalties published by HUD for various violations by landlords, including non-compliance with FHA:[10]

Description	Statutory Citation	Regulatory Citation (24 CFR)	Previous Amount	2020 Adjusted Amount
False Claims & Statements	Omnibus Budget Reconciliation Act of 1986 (31 U.S.C. 3802(a)(1))	28.10	$11,463	$11,665
Advance Disclosure of Funding	Department of Housing and Urban Development Act (42 U.S.C. 3537a(c))	30.20	$20,134	$20,489
Disclosure of Subsidy Layering	Department of Housing and Urban Development Act (42 U.S.C. 3545(f))	30.25	$20,134	$20,489
Other FHA Participants Violations	HUD Reform Act of 1989 (12 U.S.C. 1735f-14(a)(2))	30.36	Per Violation: $10,067 Per Year: $2,013,399	Per Violation: $10,245 Per Year: $2,048,915
Multifamily & Section 202 or 811 Owners Violations	HUD Reform Act of 1989 (12 U.S.C. 1735f-15(c)(2))	30.45	$50,334	$51,222
Lead Disclosure Violation	Title X—Residential Lead-Based Paint Hazard Reduction Act of 1992 (42 U.S.C. 4852d(b)(1))	30.65	$17,834	$2,048,915
Section 8 Owners Violations	Multifamily Assisted Housing Reform and Affordability Act of 1997 (42 U.S.C. 1437z-1(b)(2))	30.68	$39,121	$39,811
Lobbying Violation	The Lobbying Disclosure Act of 1995 (31 U.S.C. 1352)	87.400	Min: $20,134 Max: $201,340	Min: $20,489 Max: $204,892
Fair Housing Act Civil Penalties	Fair Housing Amendments Act of 1988 (42 U.S.C. 3612(g)(3))	180.671(a)	No Priors: $21,039 One Prior: $52,596	No Priors: $21,410 One Prior: $53,524
Manufactured Housing Regulations Violation	Housing Community Development Act of 1974 (42 U.S.C. 5410)	3282.10	Per Violation: $2,924 Per Year: $3,654,955	Per Violation: $2,976 Per Year: $3,719,428

Table 1. Source: *https://www.govinfo.gov/content/pkg/FR-2020-03-06/pdf/2020-04146.pdf*

Federal courts may also award punitive damages when there is clear evidence of willful or malicious intent, as well as attorney fees to the prevailing party. You also could be the subject of an injunction, and—just to add insult to injury—HUD maintains public records of all charges (available back to 2004, including press releases, complaint details and landlord information).[11]

PREMISES LIABILITY

"Premises liability" refers to the complex array of state codes and case law that, collectively, hold a property owner responsible for damages arising from incidents occurring on his or her property. Some legal principles of premises liability are fairly consistent across all 50 states; for example, owners who occupy a property must make reasonable efforts to maintain a safe environment for invited visitors. Breach of this duty typically results in legal liability. Some of the more common situations that trigger premises-liability litigation include:

Dog Bites   Slip-and-Falls   Construction Hazards

Pools/Jacuzzi   Inadequate Maintenance   Exposed Wires

Children   Crimes by Third-Parties   Insufficient Security

What happens when injuries occur at a rental property? Historically, landlords had reduced responsibilities for the guests of tenants, as tenants are presumed to be in control of the property condition. However, there are situations in which the landlord, and not the tenant, is primarily responsible (legally, if not morally) for the condition leading to a claim of damages. Despite all of the slight differences in state statutes and case law, there are some key principles of premises liability that are generally applicable to most landlords.

First, many states focus on the status of the person injured on the property, usually described as an *invitee* (invited customer on a commercial property), *licensee* (invited social guest) or *trespasser*.[12] For the first two categories, the invitation comes with an implied promise that the property is safe to visit. Therefore a higher duty of care is owed to these individuals. On the other hand, traditional laws imposed little or no liability for trespassers, other than a duty to not intentionally harm (for example, setting a trap). A common exception to trespasser liability involves children: landlords owe a higher duty of care when owning an "attractive nuisance" such as a swimming pool.

Second, most states follow the concept of comparative negligence, which allows courts to assign some degree of fault on the plaintiff. If the injured party failed to use reasonable care while on a property, his or her award of damages may be reduced proportionately.

Third, regardless of the plaintiff's status on the property or his/her comparative negligence, the general trend in the law over the last 30 years is to shift the burden to landlords, allowing more and greater recoveries for victims of crimes and slip-and-fall accidents at shopping centers, hotels, office buildings and apartment communities (you are probably familiar with some of the more outrageous examples of premises litigation, like burglars suing for dog-bite injuries.)

The traditional approach required plaintiffs to prove 1) that a dangerous condition existed, 2) that the condition caused their injuries and 3) that the landlord failed to exercise reasonable care in allowing the condition to exist. Today, however, many states allow the plaintiff to merely demonstrate that there was a "foreseeable risk" of the condition occurring, based on the "mode of operation" of the property.[13] Even worse, some states (like California) effectively presume that an injury was the result of a breach of duty, and shift the burden to the property owner to prove otherwise. This stems from the California Supreme Court's view that, regardless of actual fault, "liability should often be imposed on the party, often a business, most able to implement steps that promote social welfare by enhancing safety, spreading the risk of loss and ensuring compensation."[14]

In other words, some courts promote the notion that you should pay for more than your fair share of injuries occurring on your property, simply because you have more money than your tenants or their customers.

MOLD IS GOLD
(BUT NOT FOR LANDLORDS)

Mold is big business. According to a 2018 survey of property restoration service providers, mold remediation is their second-most profitable service behind water damage repair. The average hourly charge for mold cleanup is $108 per hour![15] The restoration industry employs tens of thousands of people, with over 65% of the work being done on residential properties.[16] Most of this work is assigned through an oligopoly of eight third-party administrators who contract with insurance companies.

The restoration and remediation industry has benefited greatly from mold hysteria. As a result of numerous laws, rules and regulations promulgated in recent years, avoiding the possibility of toxic mold has led to an explosion of effort to identify and eradicate all traces of all molds of any kind, toxic or harmless, real or imaginary.

Mold—a fungus, not a plant—is found everywhere on the surface of the planet, growing on flora, soil and virtually any other substrate. Mold typically thrives in dark, damp environments. It reproduces by spreading microscopic spores into the air, which we and all animals breathe indoors and outside, every day of our lives. Many types of molds are harmless, and provide benefits ranging from decomposing dead organisms to providing the basis for antibiotic medicines. Truly toxic mold, however, can trigger serious health problems for occupants. For children and the elderly in particular, toxic mold such as *Stachybotrys atra* can be deadly. Recent cases of moldy HVAC systems in hospitals have had tragic consequences.

Whether in a residential, retail, medical or office property, mold can grow above ceilings, behind walls, under sinks or anywhere else that provides moisture (e.g., leaky window or pipe) and a nutrient-laden surface (e.g., plywood). The presence of mold need not be visible to pose a health threat or legal liability.

Whether you know it or not, there is a significant chance that mold is growing on your property now, and your tenants are possibly breathing spores from that mold. The more important questions are 1) how toxic is this mold to your tenants and 2) how extensive is the exposure? If the answer to both questions is "very", then you may have a significant risk of legal liability. This may be true even if your tenants caused the initial conditions that invited the mold, such as a toilet flood, burst water bed, broken window, etc.

Not surprising, California has been on the forefront of creating liability traps for landlords with respect to mold. Some cities like San Francisco also have their own mold-related regulations for rental property owners. But regardless of the state, tenants everywhere can sue their landlords for alleged health problems and other damages relating to toxic mold.[17] These cases regularly lead to large settlement agreements. As previously mentioned, even if a mold issue does not lead to litigation, the remediation process can be quite costly.

A NOTE ABOUT ARBITRATION CLAUSES

One of the few tools for landlords to mitigate the risk of costly litigation is to require arbitration. This is achieved through common, boilerplate arbitration clauses in lease agreements. In a typical arbitration clause, a tenant agrees to submit a claim arising from the lease to an arbitrator (or arbitration panel), rather than going directly to court. Many contracts reference the rules of the American Arbitration Association, which govern complaint procedures, discovery, fees, hearings, jurisdiction, timing and awards.[18] This approach can save time and money (though arbitrations are by no means "cheap"), and deter meritless or harassing lawsuits.*

In recent years, however, the plaintiffs' bar has set its sights on arbitration clauses, seeking to force more and more disputes into court. Arbitration, as it turns out, is bad business for trial

---

* Landlords generally should not use arbitration clauses for eviction, as most states will require a shorter timeframe for resolution than arbitration.

attorneys, as arbitrations result in fewer billable hours and often have lower awards from which to claim percentage-based fees. Class-action lawsuits clearly illustrate this dynamic—class members receive token awards or even coupons, while law firms can rake in millions of dollars in fees.

In September 2019, the U.S. House of Representatives, under the considerable influence of the powerful trial-attorney lobby, passed the "Forced Arbitration Injustice Repeal Act", which would ban private pre-dispute agreements that require arbitration of certain employment, consumer and other business disputes.[19] Although this version of the bill will be vetoed, a future version certainly could pass under a combined Democratic-controlled White House and Congress.

More alarming for landlords is a 2018 California Court of Appeal case, *Weiler v. Marcus & Millichap*, providing yet another example in a long history of judicial activism in the Golden State.[20] In *Weiler*, the court greatly eroded the ability of landlords to contractually require all residential tenants to participate in arbitration. Specifically, the court held that a party may be excused from an arbitration agreement he signed on the basis that he cannot afford sharing the costs of an arbitration panel (because county judges are free and private arbitrators are not)! In a landlord-tenant dispute, under *Weiler*, the landlord would have to agree to pay all of the arbitrator fees in order to compel a tenant to comply with the arbitration.

As California is often on the "cutting edge" of establishing new public-policy rationales for voiding contracts, other states likely may follow this approach. You can expect to see tenants increasingly claiming "impoverishment" in advance of arbitrated disputes.

CHAPTER 3A

Investment Analysis 101:
Your Rental Property May No Longer Be a Great Investment

DON'T KEEP UP WITH THE JONESES
THEIR MATH IS WRONG

In 1978, Billy and Betty Jones bought a deep, narrow lot in Costa Mesa, California. At the time of purchase, the lot held a single structure: a dilapidated shack dating back to the orange-grove era. By the late '70s, the neighborhood in question had become densely populated via a mix of one- or two-story garden-style apartments and townhomes. Billy and Betty astutely recognized the opportunity to transform the parcel into a six-unit rental complex. By the time the Joneses had purchased the lot, completed the permitting process, torn down the existing structure and constructed the new apartments, it was 1980 and they had spent a total of $500,000, most of which came from a loan of $400,000.

By 2010 their loan was paid off. They had spent another $100,000 on improvements and replacements over the years, bringing their total capital costs to $600,000 (not including the interest on the loan).

Jump again to 2019, and the Joneses—now well into their retirement years—are earning a net monthly income of $10,000, or $120,000 per year from their six-unit complex. That is a pretty good cash flow for an investment of only $600,000, right? After all, not accounting for inflation, the Joneses would tell you their $120,000 of income represents a 20% annual yield.

Unfortunately, the Joneses' perspective is completely wrong. And this is not an uncommon mistake. We often meet clients who fail to understand the difference between their current yield ("Equity Yield Rate") and the far-less-relevant yield that the Joneses are touting.

Every day, you make a decision to sell or keep an existing investment, whether it be a stock, bond or rental property. This may not be a conscious decision, but you make it nonetheless. By keeping an investment, your action suggests you continue to believe that this asset represents your best available option for the class or sector to which the asset belongs. Put another way, you ostensibly are not selling the asset because there is no available investment opportunity with a similar risk profile that will produce a higher return. After all, if you knew that you could replace any investment with something similar but better, you would be silly not to. At least in theory.

Yet millions of seemingly smart, sensible people engage in such behavior on a daily basis, often for years or decades. They roll over the same low-yielding CD at their bank every year, despite dozens of ads for higher-yielding CDs. They let the same mutual fund sit in their IRA for years, despite there being 20 funds in the same category with a higher Morningstar rating. And they continue to hold onto real estate long after—sometimes decades after—the property's yield on equity has dropped below rational levels. Usually the culprit for such irrational behavior is not mental deficiency, but lack of knowledge.

Returning to Billy and Betty Jones, what we did not mention yet is that in 2019 they received an offer from a developer in the amount of $3.2 million to purchase (and tear down) their rental property. Despite knowing this, the Joneses refused to sell because, in their words, "Where else would we get a 20% annual yield on our money?"To which we reply, after taking a deep breath, "BUT YOU ARE NOT GETTING A 20% YIELD!"

What, then, is their real current yield (Equity Yield Rate)? The math is actually fairly simple. We divide their annual cash flow (net income before taxes and depreciation over 12 months)* by the current equity:

JONES RENTAL PROPERTY YIELD

Annual Cash Flow	$120,000
(after interest, before taxes and depreciation)	
÷	÷
Current Equity	$3,000,000
($3.2 million offer less sales costs of $200k)	
= Equity Yield Rate =	**4.0 %**

Rather than focus on the $600,000 they put into their rental property, the Joneses should think about the $3 million of unrealized, but ultimately fungible, value that is wasting away, not generating adequate income. Once they understand that their asset is no longer producing the yield that other rental real estate could generate, the daily decision to keep the property starts to resemble something closer to crazy, especially if the Joneses are given actionable investment alternatives.

SIMPLE TOOL FOR ESTIMATING INVESTMENT PERFORMANCE

Okay, so it's not that simple. To use this tool effectively, you will need to know or estimate roughly 20 categories of revenues and expenses related to your rental property. A good bookkeeper or CPA already will have all of this information on hand, so ask your accounting professional before spending time generating these numbers yourself:

---

* For purposes of calculating Equity Yield Rate, we define annual cash flow as revenue minus expenses, including a deduction for interest income, but without deducting income taxes and depreciation. Here the Joneses have no loan; interest is not a factor.

Semi-Annual	H1					
Quarterly	Q1			Q2		
Monthly	Jan	Feb	Mar	Apr	May	Jun
REVENUES						
Rental Income						
Other Fees						
TOTAL						
EXPENSES						
Interest Payment						
Property Management						
Water/Sewer						
Trash						
Landscape/Gardening						
Facility Maintenance						
Security						
Unreimbursed Electricity						
Marketing						
Unit Turnover Costs						
HOA Fee						
Repairs/Replacements						
Owner Association Dues						
Bookkeeping/Tax Prep						
Insurance						
Ad Valorem Property Tax						
Local Fees/Assessments						
Legal						
Personal Time						
Other						
TOTAL						
CASH FLOW						

Table 2.

H2					
Q3			Q4		
Jul	Aug	Sep	Oct	Nov	Dec

Revenue Sub-Total

X Occupancy Rate

= Total Annual Revenues

To have a meaningful final annual revenue number, it must reflect your estimated vacancy over the next ten years. For example, if you think the property will be vacant 5% of the time between tenants, multiply the subtotal by an occupancy rate of 0.95 to reach a final Total Annual Revenue number.

Total Annual Expenses

Annual Cash Flow

Under "REVENUES", be sure to capture all of your income. For example, you may have a base rent plus a pet fee. Or perhaps you have a shared utility expense that you allocate to individual tenants. Do not forget to adjust for vacancies, as noted previously.

Under "EXPENSES", we have a few explanatory notes to help you achieve the most accurate results:

Interest Payment

Do not include your entire loan payment if it is amortized. Only include the portion of your payment that is attributable to interest.

Property Management

Be sure not to miss—or double-count—expense items that your property manager pays for and includes in your bill. The best approach is to only include your manager's percentage fee here, and add any itemized items to one of the other categories.

Water/Sewer/Trash

This is intended for any utility bills you pay that are not paid or passed through to the tenant(s).

Landscape vs Facility Maintenance

Our intent here is to separate what you may pay for lawn/gardening/tree care from other types of regular maintenance, such as plumbing, electrical, HVAC maintenance, painting, etc.

Security

Security could include anything from an external webcam to an onsite guard.

Unreimbursed Electricity

To the extent that you pay for any electricity on the rental property that is not billed to your tenant(s), include that here.

Marketing

This includes the cost of classified ads for vacancies or any referral fees.

Unit Turnover Costs

Depending on the situation, this could include any number of expenses, but typically includes:

- Cleaning
- Painting
- Locksmith
- Property manager's re-tenant fee
- Background check (net of application fee)

Homeowners Association Fee (HOA) Fee

This is self-explanatory. Include any HOA fee related to your rental property.

Repairs/Replacements

Include any and all "big ticket" items you anticipate spending money on (or recently incurred).

Owner Association Dues

If you belong to a local apartment owners' group, for example, include this as landlord expense (if you have multiple properties, allocate the dues to each property).

Bookkeeping and Tax Prep

Include all of the billable hours relating to your rental property.

Insurance

You may have multiple insurance policies or riders covering different risks. Ask your broker for a breakdown if you are not certain about your coverages and your premiums.

Ad Valorem Property Tax

This is the tax that is based solely on the adjusted value of your property. In California, for example, this number is based on 1% of your original purchase value, increased no more than 2% per year. The *ad valorem* tax is typically the largest single item on a residential tax bill.

Local Fees/Assessments

In addition to the ad valorem tax, you likely have line items on your tax bill for special taxes, fees, bond payments and special assessments. In some locations, especially for commercial properties, the bond fees and special assessments may add up to more than the *ad valorem* tax.

Legal

Estimate any expenses and billable time you may have regarding eviction costs, document review and litigation.

Personal Time

Divide your total gross annual income by 2,000. The resulting number is a fair estimate of the economic value of one hour of your time. If your personal annual income is $100,000, then your hourly rate is $50.00. Next, estimate your monthly time spent working on your rental property. For example, if you are spending 20 hours per month doing ANYTHING related to your property—from paying bills to mowing the lawn—include the time. Finally, multiply that total monthly time by your hourly rate. The final number is your monthly personal time expense. In the example here, $50.00 x 20 hours = $1,000/month, or $12,000 per year.

———————————————

Now that we know the annual cash flow from your rental property, we have one final number to plug into the equation: your current property value, less any outstanding loans and projected sales costs (i.e., equity).

The most accurate version of this number would be based on an actual purchase offer. In the absence of a willing buyer, the next best estimate is that of an appraiser, who will consider factors such as local comparable transactions, the property's replacement cost, the estimated capitalization rate for similar rental properties and other data to produce an estimated value. Or, for our purposes, you can just give it your best guess. Whatever the source, you must then adjust the value to reflect your outstanding mortgage and sales costs. In the formula below, "Current Equity, Net of Sales Costs" refers to the value of a property, reduced by 7% (or multiplied by 93%), less the loan balance.

Finally, to determine your Equity Yield Rate, insert the numbers here:

_____	÷	_____	=	_____
Annual cash flow		Current Equity, Net		Equity Yield Rate
(After interest, before taxes)		of Sale Costs		

Here's an example:

$28,000	÷	**$697,500**	=	**4.01%**
Annual cash flow		Current Equity, Net		Equity Yield Rate
(After interest, before taxes)		of Sale Costs		

We will come back to your current yield on equity multiple times in this book, but in the absence of your own number, we will refer to the 4% yield example above.

This page intentionally left blank

CHAPTER 3B

Investment Analysis 102:
How Do You Know if Something Else is Better?

YOU KNOW YOUR ACTUAL YIELD—NOW WHAT?

This chapter—and indeed this entire book—is predicated on the assumption that you own rental real estate because you like income. Otherwise, you would invest all of your money in tech stocks or commodities. We, the authors, like income too. We believe strongly in the historic ability of real estate assets to deliver higher risk-adjusted returns while also providing a source of long-term appreciation. Further, in the United States real estate ownership is supported by public policies and tax rules that are potentially more favorable than other types of asset classes. For all of these reasons and more, our discussion of replacement options for your real estate investment is limited to the real estate universe.

Let us suppose that your current Equity Yield Rate from the previous page is 4%. The next question, then, is whether you realistically could replace your property with another real estate investment that:

- has a similar or better risk profile,
- is paying the same or higher Equity Yield Rate, and

• has similar or better expectations for appreciation.

You may be thinking, why would I replace my current property with a property that has the same risk profile, same yield and same likelihood of appreciation? Obviously, the goal would be to improve on at least one or two of those factors. However, all things being equal, such a property could have other beneficial attributes that are difficult to quantify, such as making your life easier. We will touch on this again later in the book.

Risk Profile

When we use the term "risk profile", we are referring to the categorical risks of owning any real estate investment. We delve deeper into some of these risks later, but here are the main examples:

- Macroeconomic risks
  - » Recession
  - » Interest rates
  - » Inflation
  - » Unemployment
- Regional economic risks
  - » Supply/demand
  - » Demographic shifts
- Governmental risks
  - » Zoning
  - » Taxation
- Tenant-related risks
  - » Concentration
  - » Business/industry exposure
  - » Occupancy
  - » Litigation
- Operational risks
  - » Expense control
  - » Casualty
  - » Capital expenditure
  - » Obsolescence

Like thumbprints, no two properties have the exact-same risk profile, but most investors have a "comfort zone", based on their ability (or believed ability) to assess the risks of property ownership. Many investors start with residential rental property and work their way up to multi-unit apartment complexes. Their past experience with smaller residential deals gives them confidence to understand the risks of larger, but similar, properties. Other people venture into property types related to their past business or employment experience, such as small retail or office properties. Some sophisticated (or well-advised) investors will venture into several types of real estate, relying on underwriting principles that apply to all rental properties.

When comparing the risk profile of two properties—for instance, the property you own now and another that you are considering to replace it—it is important not to disregard the risks to which you are currently exposed, despite the lack of incidents to date. A classic example is the California-based investor who expresses undue concern for tornadoes or blizzards in the Midwest, despite living in a California valley that is prone to fires, flooding and devastating earthquakes. To wit, on a scale of 15 (lowest risk) to 65 (highest risk) RealtyTrac gives San Diego County a natural-disaster risk score of 45 ("Very High"), compared to 25 ("Low") in Dallas County, Texas.[21] If a California investor's rental property has not yet been burned, flooded or toppled, she may be more afraid of a Caribbean hurricane than a San Andreas temblor.

Whether a potential replacement property is across town or across the country, any difference in perceived risk should be viewed in the context of total investment return (there is nothing wrong with accepting a new or higher risk when making an investment, provided you are being properly compensated for such risk). You may demand a higher return from a hotel redevelopment project in Detroit than a class-A apartment community in Atlanta, because the risk of investing in the former seems much higher.

As we use the term, your "total investment return" comes from two sources: 1) the income you receive during ownership of a property, also known as "yield", and 2) the appreciation you realize upon its sale. Income is more important to our clients, so we will address yield first.

Equity Yield Rate

To estimate the current Equity Yield Rate you would receive from a property available on the market, you would start by determining its "cap rate", short for capitalization rate (often this figure is provided in the broker package for the marketed property). Describing properties as having a "cap rate" reflects the importance of cash flow in assigning value to investment real estate. The term "cap rate" has evolved to have two related but different meanings, and you should understand both the "broad" and "narrow" usages.

Broad use of "cap rate"

Reporters and analysts often will describe the average "cap rate" or "cap" for a given type of property in a given market. For example, they might say, "Class A office in the CBD is trading at a 5-cap". Translated from broker speak, this means that all of the newer office buildings with modern amenities, in the central business district, that sold recently, were purchased at an average price in which the projected 12 months of net operating income (without factoring loan servicing, depreciation or taxes) for each property was 5% of said price.

Another way of expressing the broad use of cap rate is to say that, for a given property type in a particular area, investors are expecting to receive a specific stream of income. Much like bond yields, differences in cap rates over time and geography are a function of interest rates, available investment capital and the varying actual or perceived risks associated with each property type. Cap rates can be described locally or nationally, for different sectors of real estate and for different classes (A, B, C, etc.). As another example, you might see a chart for historic cap rates of all class-B apartments in Nashville. If a 20-year old suburban Nashville apartment complex produces a relatively stable income over time, but the cap rates for all similar properties in Davidson County go up, then the market value of the property almost certainly will go down. Cap rates, in other words, are the inverse of price.

Narrow use of "cap rate"

When a broker describes the cap rate of a particular property, he usually means the projected 12-month net operating income of the property divided by the listing price. These are both estimated numbers, as the property could ultimately trade at a different price, and the real income a year later may turn out to be higher or lower than the broker's pro forma.

Nevertheless, let us assume that the broker's marketing package has an accurate projection of revenues and expenses, and that you plan to offer the asking price for a property. The cap rate quoted by the broker equates to Net Operating Income/Purchase Price.

Now there is one more step for calculating Equity Yield Rate, because there is an additional financial factor unique to you: leverage.

Quite sensibly, brokers and analysts reference cap rates, rather than Equity Yield Rate, because the amount of debt an investor employs to purchase a property will be different from owner to owner. Cap rates allow for an apples-to-apples comparison of properties in the marketplace. In your case, however, we are looking to compare oranges to oranges.* Your current orange is the property and loan you have today, while the new orange is another property with the same amount of debt (perhaps with a different rate of interest).

To determine your estimated yield from a potential acquisition—and compare that yield with your current property—we

---

* To be even more accurate in comparing your yield to that of a marketed property using a projected NOI, adjust your 12-month cash flow to reflect a projected estimate.

need to know the following variables, (A and B can be copied from the prior spreadsheet):

Your property value, net of sales expenses**: $_____(A)
Loan balance of your property**: $_____(B)
Estimated interest rate on new loan: %_____(C)
Advertised cap rate of new property: %_____(D)

Assuming that the new property will have the same leverage (ratio of debt to value) and initial value as your current property, and further assuming that the new loan is "interest only" during the time you plan to own the new property, we would use the following formula to calculate the estimated yield for the new investment property:

$$\frac{\text{Current Equity}}{\text{Yield Rate}} = \frac{(A \times D) - (B \times C)}{(A - B)} \quad \frac{(\text{Yield after loan interest})}{(\text{Equity})}$$

Let us suppose your rental property would net $1 million upon sale, and you have an outstanding loan balance of $500,000. You intend to buy another (hopefully better) property for the same price, using the same amount of debt. The property you are eyeing is marketed with a cap rate of 5%, meaning the net income would be 5%, or $50,000, before accounting for loan payments or taxes. We will use 4% as the new interest rate (at the time of writing this book, 4% is entirely possible).

Here is how you would plug in these numbers:

Your property value, net of sales expenses: $ 1,000,000   (A)
Loan balance of your property: $ 500,000   (B)
Estimated interest rate on new loan: 4.0   % (C)
Advertised cap rate of new property: 5.0   % (D)

$$\text{Current Equity Yield Rate} = \frac{(\$1{,}000{,}000 \times 5\%) - (\$500{,}000 \times 4\%)}{(\$1{,}000{,}000 - \$500{,}000)}$$

$$= \frac{(50{,}000) - (20{,}000)}{(500{,}000)}$$

$$= \frac{(30{,}000)}{(500{,}000)}$$

Current Equity Yield Rate =   6.0%

After walking through the math, you can appreciate why a cap rate is a property-driven figure, while a yield is a personal cash-flow number. Your yield for a given property will be different than another owner's yield, depending on the amount and terms of your loan.

In the above example, your personal yield would be higher than the property's advertised cap rate, because you are (i) borrowing money, at (ii) an interest rate that is lower than the cap rate. You may have noticed that the denominator in the yield calculation is the purchase price minus the loan amount. In other words, your yield is based on the actual amount you invested out of pocket—your equity—rather than the full purchase price, part of which was paid by a bank in the form of a loan. Of course, if you do not plan to borrow any money to buy a property, then the cap rate and the current yield will be the same number.

Later in the book, we will cover pre-packaged investment programs that already have financing in place. In these programs, the sponsors of the real estate deals have already done the yield math for you. If you know the yield on your current property, you can easily compare it to the yields of these other programs.

Note: what we call Equity Yield Rate often will be referred to as "Cash on Cash Distribution". The two numbers are equivalent at the outset of a new investment; however, we prefer Equity

---

** If you are not replacing your rental with the same value and debt amounts, estimate those amounts for the new property.

Yield Rate because it tracks your yield as a function of current value, while looking backward at first-year cash-on-cash numbers becomes increasingly inaccurate over time.

Speaking of backward, one final word on Billy and Betty Jones. As you may recall, they thought they were earning a 20% yield, until they did the math correctly and realized their current yield was only 4%. Because the Joneses no longer have any outstanding debt on their property, they could sell their rental units and buy another property "at a 5-cap" to increase their annual income from $120,000 (4% of $3MM) to $150,000 (5% of $3MM). To enhance their yield even further, they could purchase a "5-cap" property with a 50% loan at 4% interest rate, resulting in a 6% yield, or $180,000 of annual income (we will discuss the benefits and risks of leverage in a later chapter). By borrowing 50% and bumping up from a "4-cap" to a "5-cap" property, the Joneses could increase their income by $60,000 per year.*

APPRECIATION

We all know that humanity "cannot live by bread alone", and while income is the daily bread of real estate, appreciation is the butter. Or jam. Or plant-based butter substitute. You get the idea.

Volumes are written on this subject, but the appreciation of investment real estate is driven primarily by just a few interrelated factors:

Cap Rates

The annual net operating income that investors expect to receive from a particular property type in a given geographical area—a function of interest rates, operating risk and availability of investment capital.

Supply and demand

Availability of similar property types in a given area, relative to the need or desire in the area for that property type.

---

*Juicing performance with debt is a two-way street. See Chapter IX.

Path of progress

Demographic or zoning changes in a given geographic area that cause a significant change in demand for either 1) the current use of the property or 2) a different use to which the property could be adapted.

Describing real estate appreciation in the United States is like talking about the weather in national terms. A chart of the average temperatures in the contiguous 48 states is not very meaningful to someone living in Fargo or Miami or Phoenix. Indeed, the temperature difference between Corona Del Mar, California and Corona, just 25 miles inland, can be 30 degrees in the same moment (the difference in housing prices is even greater). In real estate, while location clearly is a driving factor in investment performance, we nevertheless can glean important information from nationwide pricing data, as we all are subject to the same macroeconomic forces to some degree.

The chart below comes from data provided by CoStar, a leading provider of commercial real estate information, analytics and online marketplaces. CoStar uses an index of representative properties' repeat sales history to demonstrate the change in values of investment real estate, generally, across the United States over time:[22]

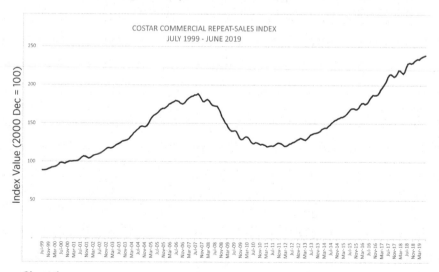

Chart 1.

Over the 20 years covered by this chart, commercial real estate values increased by 170%, which equates to 8.5% per year on a non-compounding basis. If you start with the last peak in prices (August 2007), the return is a more modest 27% over 12 years, or roughly 2.25% per year non-compounding. In the worst scenario on this chart, aggregate prices dropped between July 2007 and March 2011 a total of -36%, or -9.6% per year. Clearly, anyone who bought and sold investment real estate during the latter period likely experienced negative appreciation, though there are exceptions to trends in all markets at all times.

Data like the above chart provided by CoStar can be sliced-and-diced even further, specific to different types of real estate, of varying classes, in different markets. Despite the dozens of nuanced variations between these data sets, they all follow the same basic pattern shown above: an apex in 2007, a nadir in 2011, and a return to 2007 values by 2017 (with the exception of apartments, which had recovered in early 2015). Among the four major property types—office, industrial, retail and apartments— apartments performed best over this time, while retail was just behind office as the worst performer in terms of appreciation.

So, what caused the boom and bust of the early 2000s? This is the topic of much academic discussion and some debate, all of which is outside the scope of this book. Nevertheless, here is the briefest of summaries. In a relatively low interest-rate envi- ronment, too much capital was chasing real estate of all types in all locations, especially in the single-family residential market. This triggered over-building in places like Las Vegas, Phoenix and the Inland Empire of Southern California. At the same time, Internet shopping ramped up rapidly, eating into traditional retail sales and resulting in complete disruption, if not devastation, of malls and many retail chain businesses ranging from book sales to video rentals to electronics. Office parks built in the '80s and '90s ran out of parking spaces as the worker-per-square foot ratio accelerated, due to the massive floor space being reclaimed from ever-shrinking office machinery. Industrial real estate certainly felt the temporary effects of the economic slowdown, but did not experience the same paradigm shift that retail continues to experience today; this explains why industrial properties exhibited the shallowest peak-to-trough change among the major sectors of real estate. Apartments bounced back most quickly, as they are the only sector of investment real estate that provides a fundamental human need: shelter.

When the inherent flaws in the subprime mortgage market were finally exposed, the resulting bankruptcies, bailouts and freeze on investment capital whipsawed the entire real estate market. A subsequent drop in oil prices also contributed to the duration of the real estate recovery in Houston and other energy-dependent markets. And all of this occurred at a time when a naturally-recurring recession was likely already underway, which the real estate crash arguably pushed into the "Great" category. When investors perceive increased uncertainty in the real estate market, that risk is reflected in the higher yields that investors will require to compensate for assuming said risk. This phenomenon was pronounced and widespread during the Great Recession.

To illustrate this concept, we consider Joe the pension adviser. Suppose Joe works for a large California pension fund. On behalf of the fund, Joe is considering buying an office building in downtown Oklahoma City. During his due-diligence process, Joe wakes up and reads in the Wall Street Journal that oil prices dropped by 40% in the last week. Immediately, Joe calls his colleagues and, after some discussion, they agree that this news heightens the risk that some tenants in the office building could default on their lease payments (or move out when current leases expire). Whether right or wrong, Joe notifies the seller's broker that they will be demanding a cap-rate increase of 0.10% (say, from 6% to 6.1%) for this and all similar properties, despite the fact that projected revenues from the Oklahoma City office building are virtually fixed for the next few years. Just like that, the market value of the property dropped because the cap rate, a function of risk driven by uncertainty, ticked up by 10 basis points.

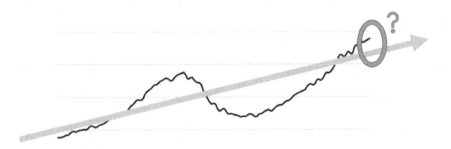

What lessons about real estate appreciation can we learn from the ups and downs of the last 20 years? First, it is evident that in our complex, highly-regulated and interdependent economy, no real estate is an island (unless, of course, you actually own an island). Second, it seems that the aggregate real estate investment market has followed a general upward trend, with average prices landing in 2017 in roughly the place they would have been if the trend line from 1999-2003 had continued sans bubble. Finally, if this over-simplified analysis holds true, we likely will see another reversion to the mean, whose magnitude depends on how far we deviate from the trend line in the coming years.

INTERPLAY OF YIELD AND APPRECIATION

Because cap rates—and therefore prices—are often more volatile than occupancy rates or rental rates, we find that estimating income is more reliable than projecting appreciation. For example, in a triple-net lease (where the tenant pays all maintenance, insurance and tax expenses under a formulaic rent schedule), a landlord can project her income for the next five years to the penny, without having a strong sense of what the property's market value will be at the end of that time.

One way to increase the chances of appreciation is to increase one's rental revenue. Although landlords have very little control over cap rates or the regional supply of similar properties, they certainly can influence demand by making their property more attractive. This can be achieved via operational improvements, moderate value enhancement, significant capital expenditures or some combination thereof.

To demonstrate the potential power of a well-executed "value add" strategy, we will consider the example of the Bridgetown Apartment Complex ("BAC"). Here are the specs on BAC:

- Built 30 years ago
- 100 units
- All 1- or 2-bedroom apartments
- Clubhouse with a fitness center, but dated appearance
- Good location (access to shopping and freeway)
- Average rents of $833/month ($10,000/year)
- Expense/rent ratio of 50%
- Current cap rate for this type of property: 5%

Let us pause here to test your math skills. 1) According to these given numbers, what is the net operating income ("NOI"—before income taxes, depreciation and debt service)? 2) Based on that number and the cap rate of 5%, what would be the value of the property? 3) Finally, what would be the average price per unit?

1. The average annual rent per unit is $10,000 and the expenses are 50% of that, leaving $5,000 NOI per unit. Multiplied by 100, the NOI of BAC is $500,000.
2. The cap rate is 5%. To derive a price from a cap rate, we divide the rate into the $500,000 of NOI. The result is $10 million.
3. The price per unit (or "price per door", as we say in the apartment business) is $10 million / 100 = $100,000.

Getting back to the "value add" strategy, a new investor is planning to buy BAC with 50% financing and spend an additional

$5,000 "per door" to improve the clubhouse and all of the units, as follows:

- $50,000 equity invested per door
- $5,000 additional improvements (a total budget of $500,000)

Assuming that $100,000 of the budget is spent on the clubhouse and common areas, the result is an average of $4,000 per unit. With that money, the investor will make these types of superficial improvements:

- Repaint
- Replace all dated hardware and fixtures
- Resurface kitchen cabinets
- Replace flooring
- In some units, replace older appliances

With this new "facelift", BAC now can compete with an apartment community down the road that was built only 15 years ago. Based on the average rents of the nearby property and others, the investor projects that management can increase the average monthly rent from $833 to $900 over a 30-month period. What impact would that increase in rents have on the value (appreciation) of the property?

An additional $67 per month is $804 per year. That does not sound like much, but when you divide that income by a cap rate of 5%, it equates to an increase of over $16,000 per unit! Assuming that the extra value is taxed at around 1% by diligent property tax collectors, the net increase in value is roughly $13,000. Multiplied over 100 units, the result is a total increase in value of $1,300,000.

Considering that the original investment in the "value add" strategy was an incremental $500,000, a return of $1,300,000 in less than three years—assuming the cap rate remains the same—is a very nice result. Indeed, if nothing else changed and the investor sold the property three years later, the total non-compounding return (yield and appreciation) would look something like this (not including the gradual increase in rents over the hold period):

Annual Yield @ 4% Interest-Only loan

Equity in $5,500,000   *(Purchase equity + improvements)*

Income	$ 500,000	*(Net before income tax)*
Debt service	- $ 200,000	*(4% on $5 million loan)*
Net income	$ 300,000	
Annual yield =	5.45%	

Appreciation
Orig. price	$10,000,000	
Sale price	$11,300,000	
Est. sales costs	$ 700,000	
Net gain	$ 600,000	
% Appreciation	10.90%	*(on equity investment of $5.5MM)*
Ann. Appreciation	**3.63%**	

The investor's total annualized return, then, was 5.45% from income and 3.63% from appreciation, for a combined annualized return (non-compounding) of 9.09%. Not bad.

But what if the cap rate for this property type/area had increased slightly over the three years that the investor owned the property? We can see the effect of such cap-rate changes in the table below:

Cap Rate at Sale, Three Years Later	Annualized Yield on Original Equity	Annualized Appreciation	Total Annualized Return
5.00% (same)	5.45%	3.64%	9.09%
5.10%	5.45%	2.38%	7.83%
5.20%	5.45%	1.17%	6.62%
5.30%	5.45%	0%	5.45%

Table 3. Assumes terminal NOI of $565,000. Returns are simple, non-compounding for illustration purposes only.

Remember, cap rates are essentially the inverse of property values relative to income. Despite increasing BAC's annual income by 13%, the investor would not realize any gain (after sales costs) if the cap rate increased by 30 basis points in three years. While this may seem disappointing, the result illustrates the importance of revenue, and the ability to increase revenue over time, when future cap rates are uncertain. As we will see later on, the results of "decompressing" cap rates are worse when a property exhibits little or no revenue growth.

Which brings us back to your property. Now that you understand your current yield and have the ability to determine your potential yield upon owning another property, you can pair that knowledge with awareness of risk and some sense of what drives appreciation. Further, if it is likely that the same types of risks and drivers of long-term appreciation are going to affect your property and another property equally, then comparing yield becomes a highly determinative factor in your decision to replace your property with another investment. In other cases, the risks and economic factors affecting an alternative property may be too different to rely heavily on yield, and may require more investigation and professional guidance.

A side note about single-family residential ("SFR") rentals:

A good number of real estate investors "backed into" being a landlord by holding on to a home they originally purchased as their personal residence. Some of these folks—you may be one as well—got the investment "bug" and bought more SFRs as rental properties. We know plenty of people who are wealthy today from this very strategy.

Unlike traditional commercial real estate, historic SFR appreciation is tied much more closely to neighborhood home values than to cap rates of small apartments. This is largely because most

SFR rentals can be sold as either an owner-occupied home or a rental. Therefore, when comparing a SFR rental to any other type of investment, it is important to pay close attention to comparable home values and retail mortgage rates, and recognize that home prices often move differently than other real estate.

This page intentionally left blank

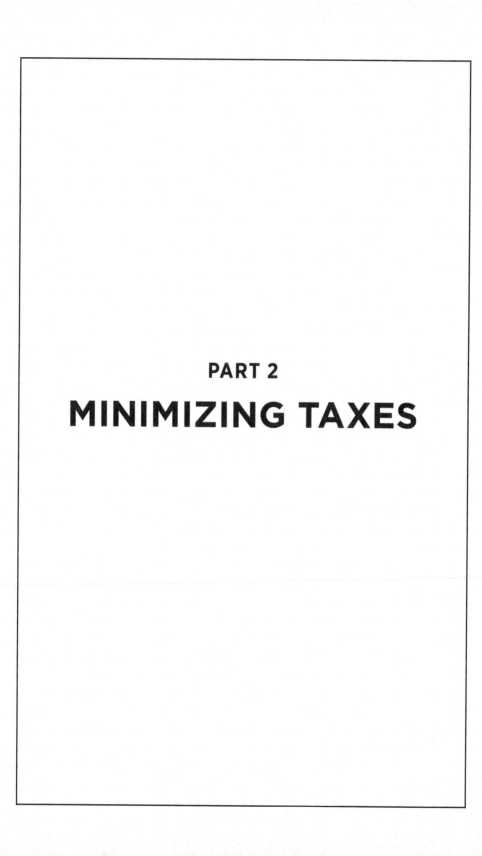

PART 2
MINIMIZING TAXES

This page intentionally left blank

CHAPTER 4

The Triple Threat of Capital-Gains Taxes:
Appreciation, Depreciation and the States

You have firmly decided to maybe consider possibly exploring the idea of perhaps selling your current property. Congratulations, this is a big first step.

If you are like most seasoned investors, the many compelling motivations to sell—landlord hassles, liability, declining investment performance—are countered by one singular obstacle: **Capital-Gains Taxes**. In this chapter, we will summarize how most people are taxed when they sell investment real estate. Chapter V will address the most common methods for deferring, and possibly avoiding altogether, the taxes we describe below.

APPRECIATION: THE CORE OF CAPITAL GAINS TAX

Too often, taxes are described in books and periodicals as if they were part of nature, no less fundamental than gravity or solar radiation. We are expected to accept taxation without question, working only to manage the effects of taxes within the system as it is given to us: "Render unto Caesar what is Caesar's", etc. (what might Matthew say today about the colossal size and scope of our local, state and federal governments?) In writing a book dealing with taxation of real estate, however, we cannot discuss the impacts of state and federal taxes on capital gains without first questioning the efficacy of such policies.

In layman's terms, a capital gain is simply the profit realized when an asset is sold, typically because the asset has appreciated in value. When you buy a nugget of gold for $500 and sell that same nugget for $1,000, presumably the nugget has appreciated (indeed, doubled in value) between the time you bought and sold it, resulting in a capital gain of $500. Regardless of whether you were lucky or smart with your timing, the government is ready to take a considerable piece of your recognized gain.

In the United States, the capital-gains tax ("CGT") goes back to 1913, when Congress quite controversially imposed a new 7% tax on all income following ratification of the 16th Amendment.[23] "Income" then included what we separately call capital gains today. Despite well-funded legal challenges to the federal income tax, the tax prevailed.[24] Over time, concepts of offsetting losses, varying brackets and duration-based levies were introduced, with the federal CGT rates ultimately treated as distinct from income tax. Today, an individual's CGT is based on 1) the length of time an asset is held and 2) the overall income of the taxpayer.

CGT is an inherently inequitable taxation scheme. First, many assets subject to CGT are already subject to corporate taxation, namely shares in corporate stock. After the corporation is taxed, our dividends as investors are taxed again, followed eventually by a final CGT upon sale.

Secondly, much of what we call appreciation is actually attributable to inflation. In real economic terms, if we recognize a gain on an asset whose value merely kept up with inflation, we have not truly experienced a gain. Yet we are taxed on the inflation.

Third, CGTs are borne disproportionately by enterprising American families who have endeavored to invest their post-tax income into assets that drive our economy—individual companies, investment funds and commercial real estate.

Finally, CGTs are asymmetrical in that all current recognized gains are taxed immediately, while offsetting losses are capped and delayed. A fair approach would allow for fully consistent treatment of both capital gains and losses.[25]

With our soapbox alighted, we turn now to the forms of CGT and their rates. Because of the fluent nature of tax rates, our desire to avoid giving tax advice, and our hope that this book will remain somewhat "evergreen" without requiring annual updates, we purposely omit the finer details of year-specific tax rates. Yet for purposes of illustration, Table 4 below describes the current state of capital-gains taxation for a *married couple*:

Taxable Income Over:	Short-Term CGT (1 year or less)	Long-Term CGT (more than 1 year)	Net Investment Income Tax
0	Same as income tax rate - taxed based on income tax bracket	0%	0%
78,750		15%	0%
250,000		15%	3.8%
488,850		20%	3.8%

Table 4. The Net Investment Income Tax applies to all income and gains.[26]

Let us employ another specific example to explain how CGT applies to appreciation realized upon the sale of real estate. In this scenario:

- Owners Jack and Jill are married with taxable income of $300,000
- They purchased a condominium for $500,000, 10 years ago, as an investment
- The property has appreciated 3% per year (non-compounding)

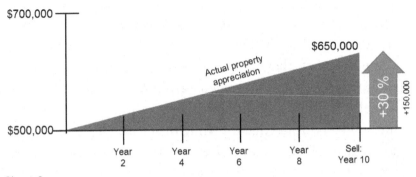

Chart 2.

Based on the above assumptions, the property has appreciated by 30% over 10 years. Jack and Jill, like most investors, understand that their realized gain—$150,000—will be subject to some form of tax upon sale. Without having any more information, we would say their CGT will be 15% of $150,000.

Current tax bill estimate: $22,500

DEPRECIATION: NOT A FREE LUNCH

As the infomercials say, "But wait, there's more!"

In addition to the actual appreciation most real estate investors enjoy over time, you also are able to account for the theoretical diminution in the value of the improvements (structures, equipment, etc. above the land) on your property. As a general concept applicable to most kinds of hard assets including real estate improvements, taxpayers can deduct the cost of an asset over its "useful life", as determined by the Internal Revenue Service, against the income earned from that asset. For example, based on IRS tables, a residential building's life is 27.5 years, meaning the original cost of the structure and other improvements can be divided by 27.5 years and claimed each year as an expense, with the same effect as other expenses related to your rental property.

Put another way, an individual owner of an apartment or rental condo can claim approximately 3.636% per year of the purchase price attributable to the "bricks and sticks" above his or her dirt.

If you buy a building for $1 million, and your accountant determines that its improvements constitute 60% of the property's value, then you can deduct 3.636% of $600,000, or $21,840, every year from your taxable passive income for the next 27.5 years. If new improvements are completed after the property is acquired, your accountant would depreciate them on a separate schedule.

Like all things tax-related, the devil is in the details. Under IRS rules, your rental property is depreciable if it meets all of these conditions[27]:

- You legitimately use the property as a rental or for your own business (e.g., not your vacation home)
- The property has improvements with a determinable useful life (i.e., a building, not a cave or hole in the ground)
- You hold the property beyond the year of purchase

As mentioned, land is not depreciable, because land does not "wear out" or "get used up". If you built your rental property, you would include the costs of clearing, grading, planting and landscaping in the cost of your land, rather than the improvements. There are exceptions, as the IRS will allow certain landscaping or hardscaping features adjacent to a building to be treated as part of the depreciable costs.

If, like most people, you purchased your rental property long after it was built, you can use the County Assessor's allocation of land/improvements as the basis for your depreciation schedule. But ask yourself how much thought anyone at the County put into calculating the value of your improvements. Probably not much. There is a good chance your accountant will find more value above ground than appears on your property tax bill. Also, the IRS allows certain closing costs to be included in the depreciable cost basis of your property, but not others. Be sure to check with your CPA.

Like all stories, claiming depreciation has a beginning, a middle and an end. Depreciation starts when your rental property is ready to be occupied. You do not have to wait until the first tenant moves in to start the clock. If you continue to operate the property as a rental, you can claim annual depreciation under the applicable IRS table for several years. It is ok if the property has periods of no occupancy, provided you were actively seeking a tenant. The story ends when you sell the property, remove it from service, or continue to own it beyond its "useful life".

Again, for most taxpayers the "useful life" of a residential property is 27.5 years, while the IRS assigns other properties a longer lifespan (typically 39 years). This assumes your accountant is using the General Depreciation System ("GDS") under the IRS's Modified Accelerated Cost Recovery System ("MARCS"). There is another table—the Alternative Depreciation System ("ADS")—that applies to non-profits, farmers and properties with limited business use. Note that certain entities like REITs must use a 40-year schedule for all real estate.[28]

If you reach the end of your rental property's useful life (nice job! 27.5 years is a long time to own a property!) your annual passive-income deductions simply stop, unless you make new improvements that can be depreciated further. More likely, you will sell the property before the end of its depreciable life. In that case, your depreciation schedule would start over on a new property— unless you do a §1031 exchange (we will come back to that later).

Now that we have a handle on depreciation, we will get back to Jack and Jill.

On the very good advice of their CPA, our friends with the $500,000 condo have been claiming depreciation on their taxes every year for 10 years. Because they own a condo with no land value, they are able to claim the entire unit as an improvement. This benefit of the tax code has allowed Jack and Jill to deduct 3.64% of $500k, or $18,200, every year. Using 40% as a rough estimate of their highest combined tax bracket, this deduction has saved our imaginary couple roughly $73,000 in income taxes since buying the condo (assuming they had earned enough passive income).

Like so many people, Jack and Jill have a good handle on appreciation but are completely clueless about depreciation. They either forgot, or never really understood, that their annual deductions come with a significant price, lurking in the shadows, waiting to strike when you least expect it:

In a less creepy analogy, recapture is when your friend buys your lunch, and says "you can get it next time", but keeps buying your lunch until you forget that you are even supposed to buy your own lunch in the first place. Then one day he hosts a dinner party and hands you the entire bill. Although the amount of the dinner bill is less than the combined costs of all the lunches he paid for, in that moment all you can think about is the shock of paying an unexpected bill. Out of nowhere, your free lunches were just—BOOM!—recaptured.

Sadly, recapture tax is far more expensive than a dinner party.

Upon the sale of an investment property, depreciation-recapture taxes often can be higher than long-term capital-gains taxes. After allowing you to claim depreciation over years for a property that actually was not depreciating, the IRS wants its money back. In all likelihood, the tax bill is less than what you would have paid in income taxes, but it is close.

This is how depreciation recapture works: each year that you claim depreciation to reduce your otherwise taxable passive income, you also reduce the "cost basis" of your original investment purchase. Cost basis is an accounting metric that starts as a real number (your purchase price) and can increase based on more real numbers (like improvements, such as a new roof or pool), but ultimately becomes fictitious after being adjusted for annual depreciation deductions.

Jill and Jack paid $500,000 in Year 1, but by Year 2 their cost basis is reduced by 3.64%* of the original price, or $18,200. After 10 years of depreciation, the cost basis (the notional amount invested in the property) is now reduced by $182,000. $500,000 (original cost basis) - $182,000 (depreciation) = adjusted cost basis of $318,000.

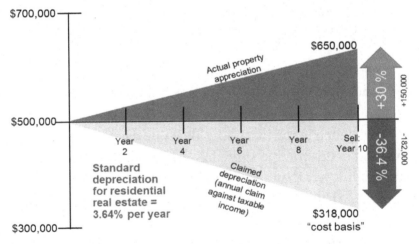

Chart 3. Amends Chart 2 by adding the effect of depreciation.

Here we see that Jack and Jill's taxable gain has grown, on paper, from an actual $150,000 to a notional $332,000. Worse, that paper gain has now pushed Jack and Jill's taxable income for the year into the highest tax bracket. For the sake of simplicity, we'll say that their gain will be taxed at a rate of 22.2%, blended between the 20%

---

* 1/27.5 = 3.6363636363%

maximum long-term gain rate and the 25% maximum recapture tax rate.

| Maximum federal rate on appreciation = | **23.8%** |
| Maximum federal rate on depreciation recapture = | **28.8%** |

Now you may be thinking, "Let's multiply 22.2% times $332,000 and get the final CGT figure." However, Congress recently enacted another tax—the Net Investment Income Tax ("NIIT")—on high-income earners like Jack and Jill. That tax adds another 3.8% to the 22.2% we estimated, resulting in a combined 26% tax on the "gain" of $332,000. Thanks to their recapture surprise and the often-overlooked NIIT, Jack and Jill's tax bill has more than tripled.

Revised tax bill estimate: ~~$22,500~~ $86,320

STATE TAXES: A MIXED BAG

As the infomercials say, "But wait, there's STILL more!"

Across the 50 states and the District of Columbia, most states impose an income tax that also applies to capital gains. Each state is different, and the tax levy can range from 0 to 13% as of the writing of this book.

On the friendly end of the scale, some states have no income tax/CGT whatsoever, while others have a small tax that does not apply to real estate investment income or capital gains.

On the other end, California not only has a high income tax and CGT, but is very aggressive about collecting it. Rather than provide a detailed table of tax rates that likely will change over time, we have included on the next page the Tax Foundation's ranking of states by income tax as of 2018.[29]

Instead of using the obvious California or New Jersey example, we will assume Jack and Jill live in a purple state with a CGT of only 4%. This tax brings their grand CGT total to 30% of $332,000.

Re-Revised tax bill estimate: ~~$22,500~~ ~~$86,320~~ $99,600

It seems unbelievable, but there it is in black and white. The original tax bill that Jack and Jill were anticipating has more than quadrupled to $100k!

State	Income Tax Rank	State	Income Tax Rank
Alaska	1	Nebraska	26
Florida	1	Mississippi	27
South Dakota	1	West Virginia	28
Wyoming	1	Rhode Island	29
Nevada	5	Alabama	30
Texas	6	New Mexico	31
Washington	6	Louisiana	32
Tennessee	8	Oklahoma	33
New Hampshire	9	South Carolina	34
Utah	10	Virginia	35
Massachusetts	11	Oregon	36
Michigan	12	Vermont	37
Illinois	13	Georgia	38
Colorado	14	Wisconsin	39
Indiana	15	Arkansas	40
North Carolina	16	Delaware	41
Kentucky	17	Iowa	42
Pennsylvania	18	Connecticut	43
Arizona	19	Ohio	44
North Dakota	20	Maryland	45
Kansas	21	DC	45
Montana	22	Minnesota	46
Idaho	23	Hawaii	47
Maine	24	New York	48
Missouri	25	California	49
		New Jersey	50

Table 5. A rank of 1 is best, 50 is worst. Rankings do not average to the total. States without a tax rank equally as 1. DC's score and rank do not affect other states. The report shows tax systems as of July 1, 2018 (the beginning of Fiscal Year 2019).

Imagine the shock of having a gain of $150,000 and having to pay 2/3 of that appreciation to the state and federal governments. TWO THIRDS!!!

To summarize the current applicable tax rates on the sale of investment real estate:

Gain Category	Cap Gains Tax	NIIT	State Tax
Appreciation	Up to 20%	Up to 3.8%	0 - 13.3%
Depreciation	Up to 25%	Up to 3.8%	0 - 13.3%

In California, a landlord in the highest tax bracket will pay:
- 37.1% tax on appreciation
- 42.1% tax on depreciation recapture

If you are a Californian with a fully-depreciated property that has doubled in value since you purchased it, you could pay a blended total tax of 39.6% of the sales price.

The collective effect of these taxes can be so impactful as to deter even the most exhausted landlords from escaping the shackles of property ownership.

Yet there is a way to diffuse the tax bomb. It is called a "§1031 exchange", and in the remainder of this book we will discuss not only tax-deferral strategies but strategies for your other ownership concerns and challenges. With some knowledge and a little help from good professionals, if suitable, you really can retire from being a landlord, regardless of your age.

This page intentionally left blank

CHAPTER 5

Tax-Deferral Basics:
Understanding the Essential Framework of §1031 Exchanges

NOTE: ALWAYS CONSULT WITH YOUR LEGAL OR TAX ADVISOR

Under IRC §1031, in a properly structured transaction, a taxpayer may sell (relinquish) a property and purchase a replacement property without having to recognize the capital gains realized from the relinquished property. A taxpayer may repeat this process multiple times, without limitation, until he or she dies. The taxpayer's heirs may sell the property after his or her death, with the cost-basis of the property being "stepped-up" to its fair market value at the date of passing. Thus a taxpayer may continue to defer, or completely avoid altogether, payment of capital-gains taxes that would otherwise be due upon the sale of investment real estate, while protecting heirs from inheriting the same tax burden.

A VERY BRIEF HISTORY OF EXCHANGE LAW

A century ago, the U.S. Supreme Court ruled that a capital gain cannot be taxed until a taxpayer actually realizes the income from the sale of the asset.[30] It may seem amazing that we needed the highest court in the country to confirm what seems like such an obvious result today. However, without confirming the concept of "realization" (aka "recognition" of gain), Congress likely would have imposed taxes on our gains before we even receive any economic benefit from appreciation!

Two years later, in 1921, Congress enacted the original law establishing "non-recognition" of income in a property transaction. Put simply, the government established the legal foundation for not recognizing a taxpayer's capital gain as being taxable, under certain conditions. This law migrated through three different sections of the U.S. codes before settling in 1954 on §1031 of the Internal Revenue Code. The original wording was limited and not entirely clear, creating volumes of judicial interpretation between the 1930s and 1990s. Much of what we consider "§1031 law" came more from the courts than from Congress. Evidently the early code sections were so ambiguous that judges, attempting to interpret the meaning of the statute, placed significant weight on the transcripts of discussions on the floor of the House.[31]

The core rationale for non-recognition of gain in a §1031 exchange—continuation of investment—is sensible and straight-forward, dating back to a 1934 report from the House Ways and Means Committee:

> [I]f the taxpayer's money is still tied up in the same kind of property as that in which it was originally invested, he is not allowed to compute and deduct his theoretical loss on the exchange, nor is he charged with a tax upon his theoretical profit. The calculation of profit or loss is deferred until it is realized in cash, marketable securities, or other property not of the same kind having a fair market value.[32]

You may wonder why we use the term "exchange" to describe selling one property and buying another. After all, in today's typical §1031 exchange, there is no direct trading of assets. The original rules contemplated transactions in which two or more parties literally exchanged assets. These early transactions had quaint names like "three corner exchange".[33]

In 1979 the Ninth Circuit, true to form, invented a new form of exchange: a transaction now could qualify for non-recognition treatment, even if the taxpayer delayed acquiring the replacement property for up to two years. This approach became known as a "Starker Exchange", after the plaintiff-taxpayer in the case.[34] (Some members of the §1031 exchange community continue to use this more specific term, interchangeable with "deferred" or "like-kind" exchanges. We prefer simply "§1031 exchange", as most people associate IRC §1031 with deferred exchanges.) Congress responded to the Ninth Circuit's judicial legislation by enacting the familiar deadlines we know today: 45 days to identify and 180 days to close. More on that later.

The U.S. Treasury Department was fairly slow to promulgate rules for §1031 exchanges. It was not until 1991 that Treasury published "safe harbors" for conducting an exchange ("safe harbor" means that, in the view of a regulating agency, you are in compliance of a statute if you follow certain guidelines that do not actually exist in the original law).[35]

As we discuss below, the most important safe harbor from the 1991 regulations, for our purposes, is the use of a "qualified intermediary" to hold the proceeds of an exchange. With this and other rules now firmly in place, taxpayers (and their agents, accountants and attorneys) could proceed with complete confidence in conducting transactions that serve to defer the payment of capital-gains taxes, by delaying the recognition of gains until a future transaction.

Since 1991, the IRS has published three additional sets of important "safe harbor rules" regarding §1031 exchanges:

- **Revenue Procedure 2000-37**
  - » Reverse exchanges and improvements

- **Revenue Procedure 2002-22**
  - » Tenant-in-Common ("TIC") interests
- **Revenue Procedure 2004-86**
  - » Delaware Statutory Trust ("DST") interests

We will reference all of these rules in later chapters.

OTHER RELATED NON-RECOGNITION RULES

§121 Exclusion: Avoiding or Reducing Tax upon Sale of Home

In 1997, Congress repealed and replaced the old "rollover" provision of §1034 with the current tax-free exclusion under IRC §121. As a result, in most circumstances you can sell your home and exclude up to $250,000 from your capital gains ($500,000 for a married couple). To qualify, you must have owned and lived in the property as your primary residence for at least a total of 24 months out of the last five years.

§1033 Exchange: Deferring Taxes upon Condemnation/Destruction

If your property is subject to an involuntary "conversion"—resulting from a governmental eminent-domain action or destruction by a natural disaster—and you realize a gain from insurance proceeds, §1033 of the Internal Revenue Code provides that, similar to a §1031 exchange, you can exchange your property on a tax-deferred basis. Some of the procedural rules of a §1033 exchange are different than §1031 and, more restrictively, the replacement property must be "similar or related in service or use" to the property that was lost in the casualty or condemnation. We cover IRC §1033 in greater detail in Chapter VII.

§453 Installment Sale: Deferring Taxes with Seller Financing

Under §453 of the Internal Revenue Code, you can sell your investment property on an "installment" basis to defer paying capital-gain taxes to future tax years, when installment payments actually are received. This strategy is also known as "seller financing". In addition to risking that the buyer may default on his/her installment payments, in a §453 sale you cannot defer your depreciation-recapture tax, which is payable in the year you sold your property.[36] See Chapter VII for more on seller financing.

In 2019, the California Franchise Tax Board announced it will impose penalties (starting in March 2020) against qualified intermediaries who fail to withhold taxes from sales proceeds when ostensible §1031 exchanges are converted into an installment note or similar arrangement, in which payments are to be paid out over two or more years.[37] This policy likely will have a considerable chilling effect on the combined use of failed exchanges and installment sales as a tax-deferral strategy in California (and other states that inevitably will adopt the same regulatory stance).

§1031 BASICS

We (the authors) own several publications regarding §1031 exchanges, including a legal text comprising several hundred pages. As with any section of the Internal Revenue Code, much has been said and written about the statutes, regulations, court cases and agency guidance, not to mention state-law issues, regarding this topic. For anyone attempting to push the proverbial envelope surrounding established rules, there is plenty of material available to generate billable hours for attorneys and CPAs. When the stakes are high enough, property owners will go to great lengths to defer paying Uncle Sam; hence, the continued publication of court cases and regulations dealing with non-recognition of capital gains.

Despite the extensive body of law surrounding §1031 exchanges, the vast majority of landlords need only be concerned with a handful of very important rules. If you follow these rules, you can defer paying CGT upon sale of your rental property:

- Proceeds of your sale must go directly to a qualified intermediary, and then directly to the seller of your replacement property.
- Your replacement property(ies) must be "like-kind" real estate. For example, you cannot buy shares of a limited partnership or REIT.*
- Upon closing the sale of your relinquished property, you must identify your replacement property(ies) within 45 days and complete the purchase within 180 days.
- Your replacement property(ies) must be of equal or greater value as your relinquished property, and you must have an equal or greater amount of equity. If your equity does not increase between your relinquished and replacement properties, you will need an equal amount of debt.**

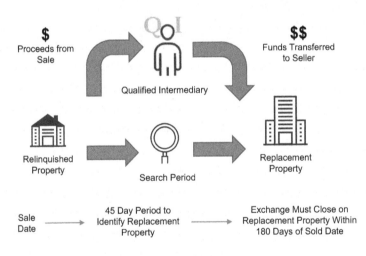

Figure 2. Diagram for a standard forward exchange.

---

* In an UPREIT, you can contribute property to a REIT in exchange for an interest in the underlying operating partnership on a one-time deferral basis. This approach has very limited applicability to most individual landlords.

** You may replace debt with additional cash, but you cannot replace equity with additional debt.

The devil, again, is in the details, but as a practical matter these rules are reasonably easy to follow, especially if you have competent people on your "deal team".

WHAT IS A QUALIFIED INTERMEDIARY AND WHY DO I NEED ONE?

IRC §1031 requires that a qualified intermediary ("QI"), also known as an "exchange accommodator", serve as the "go between" in your exchange. It is not possible to conduct a valid §1031 exchange without a QI. The QI essentially acts in an escrow capacity, but with enhanced services compared to a typical purchase/sale escrow. Once selected, your QI will perform the following functions:

- Prepare the required §1031-exchange legal documents*
- Receive, safeguard and distribute your §1031 exchange funds from the beginning to the end of the transaction
- Provide procedural guidance to you and your legal/tax advisers

Before entering into a §1031 exchange, you should select from among QIs who exhibit the following attributes:

- Excellent customer service
- Deep expertise and experience
- Reasonable rates
- Licensed attorney on staff
- Substantial insurance and fidelity bonding
- Membership in the Federation of Exchange Accommodators
- And most importantly, policies and procedures to protect your money during the exchange transaction

---

* This typically includes Escrow Instructions, a Like-Kind Exchange Agreement between the exchanger and the QI, a Trust Agreement, Assignment Agreements for both the relinquished and replacement property transactions, Identification Form and other notices/instructions.

RELINQUISHED PROPERTY THAT QUALIFIES FOR AN EXCHANGE

The following is a summary of IRS rules and regulations restricting the types of property available for tax deferral:

- Must have been "Held for Investment" (most real estate meets this requirement).
- You cannot exchange personal residential property (i.e., your home or a second vacation home—see below regarding vacation rentals).
- You cannot exchange "inventory", meaning property you purchased solely for the purpose of improving and reselling (e.g., development property, converted condominiums or "flipped" homes).
- Holding a property for at least 24 months is the safest way to establish your original intent to hold the property for investment purposes.
- The "held for investment" rule applies to both the replacement property and the relinquished property.

Exchange of Personal Property No Longer Available

As of January 1, 2018, it is no longer possible to exchange intangibles such as broadband spectrums, fast-food restaurant franchise licenses and patents; or chattel such as aircraft, vehicles, machinery and equipment, railcars, boats, livestock, artwork and collectibles. In other words, §1031 exchanges are now limited to real estate.

Although tax can no longer be deferred through like-kind exchanges of these assets, the full cost of certain tangible personal property such as vehicles, heavy equipment, farm  machinery and hotel furniture can be deducted in the year that they are placed in service, which can offset any capital gain or depreciation recapture recognized in the future. Full expensing expires in 2022, and will be reduced to 80% for assets placed in service in 2023, 60% in 2024, 40% in 2025 and 20% in 2026.

QUALIFIED REPLACEMENT PROPERTY

"Like-Kind" Real Estate

§1031 exchange rules mandate that the replacement property be "like-kind" with the relinquished property. Decades ago this was a stricter rule. Today, virtually all investment real estate is considered like-kind with the property you sold. Here are some examples of real estate that is like-kind with other investment property:

- Apartments
- Student housing
- Retail centers
- Industrial/warehouse centers
- Office buildings
- Self-storage facilities
- Hotels/motels
- Vacant or agricultural land
- Oil/gas/mineral rights
- Water/air rights
- Air rights
- Land trust properties

When assets such as apartments, hotels, and student housing are exchanged, only the real property is exchangeable. The exchange may no longer include unattached items such as furniture and equipment.

You can cross state lines to do a §1031 exchange, but you cannot exchange foreign real estate for domestic real estate. Conversely, only foreign property is like-kind with other foreign property

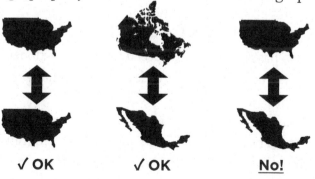

✓ OK   ✓ OK   No!

under IRS regulations.

NOT "Like-Kind": Entity Interests

Owning part of an entity that owns and operates real estate seems like direct ownership; however, the IRS distinguishes between actual ownership and entity ownership. If you sell real estate you owned directly, you cannot conduct a §1031 exchange by purchasing an interest in an entity, and vice versa. Examples of entity interests that are NOT "like kind" with real estate include:

- Limited partnerships and general partnerships
- Multi-member limited liability companies
- Corporations
- Certain vacation rentals
- REITs

In 2008, the IRS issued new guidelines for taxpayers seeking assurance that their vacation home can be relinquished in a §1031 exchange, as follows[38]:

1. You must have owned the relinquished vacation property during the prior 24-month period;
2. You must own the replacement property during the following 24-month period; and,
3. In each of the above periods, the properties:

   a) must be rented at fair-market rates to third parties for at least 14 days, and

   b) are not used by the owner for a period the greater of 14 days or 10% of the time rented to others.

FRACTIONAL REAL ESTATE INTERESTS

The IRS has approved two special forms of fractional ownership interests as qualifying property for §1031 exchanges:

- Tenant-in-Common ("TIC") interests
- Delaware Statutory Trust ("DST") interests

As noted above, if you choose one of these programs for your replacement, you must specify the dollar amount you intend to invest in a particular program.

TIC Interests

A TIC interest is an undivided interest in title, recorded directly on the property deed: "Bob Jones and Mary Smith, as Tenants in Common". All TIC owners must be a party to any loan on the property and generally will be required to hold their ownership interest in the form of a single-member limited liability company.

Whether a TIC interest qualifies as "like-kind" real estate depends on the agreement between the parties, including the real estate sponsor who put the deal together. If the agreement seems like a partnership arrangement, the TIC interest will not qualify for a §1031 exchange.

Under Rev. Proc. 2002-22 (the IRS publication that describes how a fractional interest in real estate may be deemed "like kind" for a §1031 exchange), the TIC agreement is subject to the following requirements:

- No treatment of co-ownership as an entity
- There can be no more than 35 co-owners (TIC investors)
- The co-owners are required to be involved in:
  » *hiring of any manager*
  » *creation or modification of a blanket lien*
  » *significant lease changes*
  » *disposition of the property*
- Co-owners cannot borrow from other co-owners to pay for capital expenditures

Packaged TIC programs were popular §1031 solutions in the early 2000s, but in recent years investors have gravitated toward DSTs. We address TICs in greater detail in Chapter VIII.

DST Interests

A DST is a business trust formed under Delaware state law. Chances are you have invested in a DST in the past, even if you are not familiar with the name—many mutual funds are structured as DSTs.

As an exception to the general rule that interests in business entities are not "like kind" to real estate, in 2004 the IRS ruled that an investment in a DST will qualify for a §1031 exchange. (More specifically, under Rev. Rul. 2004-86, if properly structured, the IRS ruled that a DST will be classified as a "grantor trust" for federal income tax purposes and, as a result, the purchaser of a beneficial interest in the trust will acquire an undivided interest in the property held by the DST).

Furthermore, when a DST eventually sells its real estate, an investor in the DST may re-invest his/her proceeds via another §1031 exchange.

For a DST investment to qualify as a valid replacement property under §1031, the DST:

- May only purchase real estate and short-term obligations (e.g., money market accounts)
- May not initiate additional "capital calls"
- May not renegotiate or refinance the loan; such action likely will eliminate the possibility of a future §1031 exchange
- May not renegotiate leases or enter into new leases
- May not make major improvements to the real estate
- Must distribute all cash, other than the necessary reserves, to the beneficiaries (investors)
- May not sell or exchange property and reinvest the proceeds

In light of these requirements, most DST programs invest in newer properties under a "triple net" or "master" lease, without plans for significant capital expenditures. There is only one loan, and the individual DST investors are not parties to that agreement. Investors are completely passive owners. Many DSTs are designed to sell the underlying real estate within five to ten years, at which time investors have the option to pay taxes or exchange the proceeds into another §1031-qualified property or program.

We will explore §1031 DST programs in greater depth later

in the book.

IDENTIFY AND ACQUIRE YOUR REPLACEMENT PROPERTIES

Identification Period: 45 Calendar Days

There are different rules for how much real estate you can identify as your replacement property, but no matter what you choose, you must identify your replacement property(ies) no later than 45 calendar days from the day your relinquished property closed escrow.

Again, even if your 45-day deadline falls on a weekend or holiday, there is no exception.

While it is customary to deliver the identification of your replacement property(ies) to your QI, a written statement in your purchase contract for the replacement property (subject to the content rules below) could meet the §1031 requirements.

Certain persons are disqualified from receiving your identification notice, based on their close relationship to you. Disqualified persons include a taxpayer's family member, employee, attorney, accountant, investment banker and real estate agent—especially if any of those parties provided services during the two-year period prior to the transfer of the relinquished property. To avoid identification pitfalls, it is best to work with a QI from the outset, and submit your identification notice to the QI using the QI's standard form.

You can revoke and replace your identification of replacement property(ies), provided you do so within the 45-day identification period.

Exchange Completion Period: 180 Calendar Days (or Less!)

Now that you have identified potential replacement properties for your §1031 exchange, the next step is to complete the transaction by receiving legal title to (i.e., buying) one or more of the properties you identified, no later than the earlier of:

- 11:59 pm on the 180th calendar day following the close

(sale) of your relinquished property; or

- The due date to file your federal income tax return for the tax year in which the relinquished property was sold, including any filing extensions (failing to file your taxes does not extend the §1031 exchange deadline).

In other words, you may have less than 180 days if you (or the business entity you own) sell the relinquished property in the latter half of the year.

One final comment on deadlines: it does not matter if your deadline lands on Easter or Yom Kippur or Eid Al-Fitr or Super Bowl Sunday. The IRS does not grant personal extensions for meeting timelines in §1031 exchanges. However, the President can authorize local, regional or even nationwide extensions of these deadlines.

Proper Identification

During the 45-day period following the sale of your relinquished property, you must "identify" your replacement(s). Put simply, you must deliver in writing an unambiguous description of the replacement property to a third party, subject to certain restrictions. The safest way to comply with these rules is to use a form provided by your QI and include the following information regarding the real estate you plan to acquire:

- Street address
- Legal description
- Assessor's Parcel Number (APN) if known
- Your signature (required)

According to the IRS:

The identification must be in writing, signed by you and delivered to a person involved in the exchange like the seller of the replacement property or the qualified intermediary. However, notice to your attorney, real estate agent, accountant or similar persons acting as your agent is not sufficient.[39]

Furthermore, if you identify a fractional real estate program such as a DST, many QIs will require that you also identify the name of the DST, the amount of your investment and your percent ownership in the DST.

We suggest working with your advisor and QI to ensure that your identification letter is in good order. Below is a sample of a typical ID form:

---

§1031 Exchange Identification Letter

To: (Name of Qualified Intermediary)

Relinquished Property Address: _____ **Sale Price:** _____

Client Name: _____

Method of Identification:	[ ] Three Property Rule
	[ ] 200% Rule
	[ ] 95% Exception

Identified Property	Address, City, State (include unit #)	Ownership %	Estimated Purchase Price
Property #1			
Property #2			
Property #3			
Properties #4 and above	Use attachment		

How many properties do you intend to acquire?	[ ] One (1)
	[ ] Two (2)
	[ ] Three (3)
	[ ] Other: _____ [ ] Unknown

_____   _____
Signature   **Date**

_____   _____
Signature   **Date**

(Mail, email and fax instructions and disclosures here)

The next natural question is, "How many properties can I identify?" Considering the transactional risks in buying real estate, it is better to have multiple options than to place all your bets on one property. To address this issue, the IRS allows three different methodologies for identifying multiple properties, though the first rule below is the simplest and most common.

3	**200**	**95**
Properties	Percent	Percent

Three Property Rule
- Identify up to three separate properties
- No dollar limit on the combined market value of the three properties
- Often used when you have a preference to buy just one replacement property, with two additional properties identified as "backup" options
- Can also be used when you intend to buy multiple replacements, in which case your intended allocation must be included in the identification form

Now let us suppose you plan to diversify your real estate holdings beyond three replacement properties. In that case, there are two additional rules upon which you can rely:

200% Rule
- No limit on the number of identified properties
- Combined market value of the identified properties cannot exceed 200% of the net sale price of your relinquished property
- Typically used when you have a preference to allocate your exchange proceeds across multiple properties

For example, you could identify five properties—and acquire

up to all five properties—as long as the combined market value of the identified properties (at the end of the 45-day period) is less than twice the value of the property you sold. Therefore, if your relinquished property sold for $1 million, under the "200%" rule, you could identify more than three properties, provided their combined market value did not exceed $2 million.

95% Rule

This final rule is for taxpayers who want to allocate their §1031 exchange proceeds: 1) across more than three properties and 2) for more than 200% of the sale price of their relinquished property.

- No limit on the number of identified properties
- No limit of the combined market value of identified properties
- HOWEVER, you must acquire at least 95% of the value of ALL the properties you identified

Clearly, the "95% Rule" comes with the significant risk that you may not be able to acquire 95% of the properties you identified, thereby "blowing" your exchange. But if you are VERY confident that you will be able to close, within 180 days, the transactions for all identified properties, this rule lets you pick as many properties as you want.

AVOID THE BOOT

It is possible to sell a property, conduct a §1031 exchange, buy a replacement property...and still end up paying taxes. How? The likely culprit is "boot."

"Boot" is industry jargon for any excess value you received from your exchange that otherwise should have gone into your replacement property. In order to achieve a 100% deferral of your taxes, you must completely avoid boot. Understanding the basic rules and working with experienced professionals is the best way

to eliminate boot and achieve a complete tax-deferred exchange. The three general categories of boot are as follows:

Cash/Equity Boot

The concept of cash/equity boot is very simple. To qualify for a complete §1031 exchange, 100% of the equity in your relinquished property must be used to acquire your replacement property. You can always buy more real estate, but less real estate will trigger boot, which is taxable. The rule of thumb is "always trade UP".

Debt Boot

The same principle applies to your real estate loan. Assuming you only replaced your equity, you must borrow at least as much money to acquire your replacement property as your loan balance when you sold the relinquished property. If you use all of your equity, but do not borrow as much from the bank, the reduction in debt is boot. On the other hand, if you added equity (cash from outside the exchange) to your replacement transaction, you may borrow less money, provided the total purchase value is equal or greater than the value of the relinquished property. Again, always trade up.

Certain transaction expenses related to your replacement purchase may not count towards your minimum equity and debt requirements. Common sources of disallowed purchase expenses are loan costs, which include:

- Loan fees
- Loan appraisal fees
- Lender-required inspection fees
- Prorated mortgage insurance
- Loan points

Keep in mind that disallowed expenses may constitute "boot" to the extent you have not replaced all of your equity and/or debt. As a conservative approach, treat any purchase expenses that would not exist without a loan as disallowed. If subtracting any disallowed costs from your contracted purchase price causes your net purchase amount to fall below the equity you need to replace, then you must use additional dollars to pay for the disallowed costs. Similarly, if you are financing any of the above costs with your purchase loan, double check that the loan amount, minus these costs, is greater than your previous loan (especially if you have not increased the total amount of real estate owned between your relinquished and replacement properties).

Miscellaneous Boot

If you follow the basic rules above, any boot your exchange generates should be minimal. However, to completely avoid receiving any taxable excess value, you should avoid using exchange proceeds to pay for expenses that the IRS may deem to be non-permissible transaction costs, which include:

- Prorated rents
- Tenant security deposits transferred to the buyer
- Prorated property taxes*
- Insurance payments
- Improperly released earnest-money deposits or option payments
- Any other items received that are not typical closing costs

Always review your closing statements with your tax professional!

Suppose your relinquished property sold for $500,000 and you had an outstanding loan of $200,000. Let us also assume the following types of expenses in your transaction:

- $45,000 of permissible, customary SALE expenses
- $5,000 of disallowed SALE expenses

... resulting in net funds paid to the QI of ($300k - $50k) = $250k, and

- $5,000 of disallowed PURCHASE LOAN expenses, rolled into the total loan amount.

---

* There are differing opinions on whether prorated property taxes can be paid from gross exchange proceeds without triggering boot. From a tax perspective, the safest approach is to pay the taxes separately (or at least reimburse the escrow account for the equivalent amount before the sale closes), but check with your tax professional.

In this example, the IRS total minimum replacement value is $455,000 and the minimum equity requirement is $255,000.

Here are some possible outcomes, based on the **funds paid into the replacement:**

Additional Cash from You to Escrow	$0	$0	$5,000	$5,000
Scenario:	**A**	**B**	**C**	**D**
Equity from QI to escrow	$250,000	$250,000	*$255,000	*$255,000
Purchase Loan Amount	$200,000	$205,000	$200,000	$205,000
(disallowed loan fees)	-($5,000)	-($5,000)	-($5,000)	-($5,000)
Net to Replacement Seller	$445,000	$450,000	$450,000	$445,000
BOOT	**$10,000**	**$5,000**	**$5,000**	**$0**

Table 6.

Scenario A: You have $5,000 in disallowed expenses on both sides of the transaction, for a total of $10,000 of taxable boot.

Scenario B: You have increased the loan amount to pay for the loan expenses, but did not pay for the disallowed sale expenses. The result is better than A, but still $5,000 of boot.

Scenario C: This time you did pay for the disallowed sale expenses out of pocket, but did not increase the loan amount to cover the loan expenses. Again, you will recognize $5,000 of boot.

Scenario D: Success! A completely tax-free exchange! This requires that you pay for the disallowed sales expenses out of pocket (by adding cash to escrow before your relinquished property sold) and making sure that your loan amount is $200k

---

* You may have noticed that in Scenarios C and D, the equity at the QI increased from $250,000 to $255,000. This is because the $5,000 you paid out-of-pocket—before the close of escrow on your relinquished property—actually increased the amount of money paid from escrow to the QI.

plus the $5k of loan costs (alternatively, you could pay the loan expenses out of pocket). Only in Scenario D have you met the minimum requirement of 1) replacing what the IRS considers the sale value ($455,000) and 2) replacing your minimum equity.

One final reminder about boot: every dollar of boot is taxable. We have seen people take so much cash out of their sale that it was no longer worthwhile to conduct an exchange. If you have $100,000 in gain on a $1 million property, and you decide "I'll just put $75k in my pocket", it may not be worth doing an exchange, as you already will be taxed on the $75,000 of boot and you only are deferring tax on the remaining $25,000 of gain. Put another way, why bother subjecting yourself to a §1031 exchange to acquire a $925,000 property, just to save $7,500 in taxes. Far better to exchange the entire $1 million and save $30,000 in taxes (assuming you really don't need to have an additional $75,000 sitting in the bank).

GENERAL §1031 EXCHANGE CHECKLIST

Every situation is different, but this checklist will apply to most exchanges:

X	BEFORE LISTING YOUR RENTAL PROPERTY
	Conduct a basic financial analysis of your rental
	Talk to your tax professional, establish tax consequence of sale
	Engage a §1031-exchange replacement specialist
	Verify that title is vested properly
	UPON LISTING YOUR RENTAL PROPERTY
	Engage a QI, discuss fees and procedures
	Estimate your equity and debt replacement requirements
	With your §1031-exchange replacement specialist, begin looking at potential replacement properties
	If you are planning to buy another property (as opposed to a DST or TIC interest), talk to a lender or mortgage broker

UPON OPENING ESCROW TO SELL	
	Talk to your agent and escrow officer about closing costs; with your tax professional, determine if you should pay any expenses out of pocket
	Advise escrow officer of your intent to conduct a §1031 exchange
	With your §1031-exchange replacement specialist, narrow down your target replacement properties
	Formally open an account with your chosen QI
UPON CLOSING ESCROW TO SELL	
	Verify that your escrow agent transferred all sales proceeds to your QI. Do not accept any funds from your sale
	Verify that your loan has been paid off
	Obtain a copy of your closing statement, and provide it to your QI and §1031-exchange replacement specialist
WITHIN 45 DAYS OF CLOSING SALE OF RENTAL PROPERTY	
	With the help of your tax professional and §1031-exchange replacement specialist, determine which of the property ID rules (Three Property, 200% or 95%) is applicable to your exchange
	Identify your replacement property(ies) using the form provided by your QI
	Ensure that you will be able to obtain financing, if applicable
	Verify with your tax professional that your tax filing will not inadvertently shorten your 180-day close period
WITHIN 180 DAYS OF CLOSING SALE OF RENTAL PROPERTY	
	Monitor your replacement options closely
	Purchase and close on your replacement property(ies)
	Work with your tax professional to make any required state and federal filings related to your exchange

Table 7.

Following a checklist like this, even if you have a great support team around you, will help you stay organized and reduce any stress that may arise during the transaction. Any real estate deal can be challenging, but §1031 exchanges require that you focus a little harder, especially during the first 45 days after you close on your relinquished property.

With the basics of a §1031 exchange under our belts, we turn now to the benefits of deferring capital-gains taxes, both during your life and at your passing (hopefully a long, long time from now).

This page intentionally left blank

CHAPTER 6

The Math Behind Successive Exchanges:
Swapping 'til Dropping

It is no coincidence that real estate makes up a significant portion of most wealthy families' investment holdings. Under long-standing tax law, the advantages of owning and operating real estate for investment purposes are significant. These advantages not only benefit a property's original investors but also their family members who ultimately inherit the real estate.

The two key tax advantages that apply to the vast majority of real estate investors are 1) annual depreciation deductions from taxable income, and 2) a step-up in cost basis at death. These two benefits, combined, create an opportunity for real estate investors to significantly reduce or even eliminate taxes when they are alive, then leave their real estate holdings to their children without a capital-gains tax bill.

MORE ABOUT DEPRECIATION DEDUCTIONS

Once you understand how depreciation deductions work, you may surmise that the people who wrote our federal tax laws over the last century likely owned investment real estate. The depreciation deduction is a powerful way to generate significant rental income without including all of that income on your current tax return. As we discussed in Chapter IV, this write-off is allowed because the IRS assumes that, as buildings and their fixtures age, their value declines or "depreciates". Investors are able to report this depreciation on their tax returns and apply a paper "loss" against the income they recognized as net rents. In some cases, the depreciation is equal to or greater than the net rents collected, resulting in no income tax liability in the current year.

What's more, you can claim a deduction for this supposed decline in value even while the actual value of your property is increasing! As previously mentioned, the above-ground improvements on a rental property can be depreciated (and therefore deducted from taxable income) over their "useful life", which is typically 27.5 years for residential real estate (or 3.64 % per year). Chapter IV explained how the annual depreciation deduction is like a growing bar tab at the IRS—one that you ultimately need to pay before you leave the pub. Selling your depreciated real estate without a §1031 exchange triggers a bill from the proverbial bartender, and any amount greater than your reduced cost basis will generate "recapture tax". On the other hand, repeated exchanges allow you to defer gain recognition for tax purposes, even if the cost basis of your original property is depreciated down to zero.

At first glance, this seems like merely kicking the tax can down the road. Many people, particularly those in the "Baby Boomer" generation, are inclined to pay the tax bill today, rather than have the burden of a future tax bill hanging over their heads. Perhaps they can hear their own parents quoting Benjamin Franklin: Don't put off until tomorrow what you can do today! While those words may be great advice when it comes to chopping wood for the winter, they can be terrible advice for capital-gains tax planning, for two distinct reasons:

First, the "time value of money" concept dictates that money available today is worth more than the identical sum in the future, due to its potential earning capacity. Giving your money to the IRS earlier than necessary deprives you of both the money itself and the investment income it could generate. Second, there is a powerful loophole in the tax code that could allow you to not only defer your capital-gains taxes but to actually eliminate them altogether. All you have to do is die.

STEP-UP IN BASIS

As explained in a report by the U.S. Congress Joint Committee on Taxation:

Property acquired from a decedent's estate generally takes a stepped-up basis. "Stepped-up basis" means that the basis of property acquired from a decedent's estate generally is the fair market value on the date of the decedent's death (or, if the alternate valuation date is elected, the earlier of six months after the decedent's death or the date the property is sold or distributed by the estate). Providing a fair market value basis eliminates the recognition of income on any appreciation of the property that occurred prior to the decedent's death and eliminates the tax benefit from any unrealized loss.[40]

The principle of stepped-up basis applies to real property and almost all other types of assets, with certain exceptions for interests in foreign businesses. In states that have adopted community-property law, spouses enjoy the added benefit of receiving a full step-up in basis at the death of a spouse, despite the fact that the surviving spouse owned half of the property in the first place.

Setting aside the issues related to foreign assets and deaths among spouses, giving an asset with a large difference between fair-market value and cost basis after death is generally much more advantageous (from a tax perspective) than gifting the same asset before death. For individual landlords—and their heirs—the difference can mean hundreds of thousands, if not millions, of dollars in taxes.

You may have heard the expression, "it's simple but not easy." This approach may just fall into that category. While not a tax strategy that is typically pursued with gusto, dying actually provides a potentially enormous tax benefit to your heirs. The IRS effectively rips up the old bar tab for both you and your heirs. In our industry, some folks refer to the successive-exchange approach, with the intent to hold real estate until death, as the SUD Strategy (Swap Until you Drop).

DEPRECIATION, EXCHANGES AND STEP-UP

Combining depreciation, §1031 exchanges and a step-up-in-basis strategy (dying) is one of the most common methods used by wealthy families to stay that way—for generations. Let us take a look at two scenarios to see how powerful these strategies can be when used together.

Mary bought a property 28 years ago for $250,000 and it is now worth $1,000,000. She is ready to retire and wants to sell her rental property; she intends to invest the net proceeds into a portfolio that will provide her with passive income so she can relax and travel. For illustrative purposes we will assume that the value of her investment will remain stable while she is retired. Mary's situation might look something like this:

Old Investment
- Original purchase price: $250,000
- Net sales price: $1,000,000
- Basis: $0
- Blended capital-gains tax rate: 35%
- Available for investment after taxes are paid: $650,000

New Investment
- Yield: 5%
- Resulting cash flow: $32,500
- Total cash flow after 20 years: $650,000

• Value of asset to leave to heirs: $650,000

If Mary were to pass away 10 years after the above transaction, she could leave the value of her $650,000 investment to her children and there would be no capital-gains tax liability. She had received a total of $325,000 in cash flow over the 10-year period, before her untimely demise. The combined total of the income earned and property value is $975,000.

Now let us consider a scenario where Mary uses the combined strategies of tax deferral (§1031 exchange) and step-up in basis upon death:

Old Investment
- Original purchase price: $250,000
- Net sales price: $1,000,000
- Basis: $0
- Blended tax rate: 0% (because of §1031 exchange tax deferral)
- Net available for investment: $1,000,000

New Investment
- Yield: 5%
- Resulting cash flow: $50,000
- Total cash flow after 20 years: $1,000,000
- Value of asset to leave to heirs: $1,000,000

Because of the tax deferral accomplished on the sale of the property, more money was available for investment, resulting in higher income even though the yield was the same 5% in each example. Indeed, the cash flow was more than 53% higher in the second example ($32,500 vs. $50,000)!

In addition, by deferring the taxes on the sale of the property, then benefitting from a step-up in basis, Mary was able to leave her heirs the full $1,000,000 rather than just $650,000—more than a 53% increase. Keep in mind that these examples assume zero growth after the sale of the property. If we assume a 3%-5% annual growth rate, the numbers are even more impressive.

COST SEGREGATION

Most of our discussion of depreciation has related to real estate improvements, meaning structures, hardscaping, etc. As mentioned, owners typically can deduct the depreciating value of their buildings against their income over a 27.5-year or 39-year period. In IRS parlance, depreciable buildings are known as "§1250 property".

Yet there is another category, "§1245 property", that includes equipment, furniture, fixtures and other tangible property that is depreciated over a shorter period (e.g., five to seven years). Certain types of tangible property are also eligible for accelerated depreciation (e.g., double declining balance, bonus depreciation and §179 expensing).

The rules and guidelines for depreciating §1245 property are complex and not always clear. In the words of an IRS publication:

Property allocations and reallocations are typically based on criteria established under the Investment Tax Credit (ITC) laws under §48. As a result from numerous legislative acts, court decisions and Service rulings relating to property qualifying for ITC and a lack of bright-line tests, complex and often conflicting guidance have impacted the ease in determining $1245 property from $1250 property. Related issues, such as the capitalization of interest and production costs under IRC §263A and changes in accounting method, add to the complexity of this issue.[41]

To maximize the tax benefits of depreciating tangible property acquired in the purchase of real estate, property owners often hire experts to conduct a "cost segregation" study, which is a fancy name for a list of items on the property that are not considered real estate. The allocated cost of these assets can be deducted over a much shorter timeframe (in some cases in one year), providing a potentially significant near-term reduction in taxable income.

The basic criteria for distinguishing tangible property from real property comes from the *Whiteco* case of 1975, in which the

Tax Court put forth a six-question test:[42]

1. *Is the property capable of being moved, and has it in fact been moved?*
2. *Is the property designed or constructed to remain permanently in place?*
3. *Are there circumstances, which tend to show the expected or intended lengths of affixation, i.e., are there circumstances, which show that the property may or will have to be moved?*
4. *How substantial of a job is the removal of a property and how time-consuming is it? Is it "readily removable"?*
5. *How much damage will the property sustain upon its removal?*
6. *What is the manner of affixation of the property to the land?*

For investors in industrial, medical or hospitality properties in particular, a significant amount of assets may be deemed tangible property subject to advantageous depreciation regulations. In some instances, a taxpayer may realize tax savings of hundreds of thousands of dollars after obtaining a cost-segregation study. Conversely, some properties simply do not have enough tangible assets to justify the time and expense of cost segregation.

Related to cost segregation are the potential benefits of first-year "bonus" depreciation and deductions under Internal Revenue Code §179. In the Tax Cuts and Jobs Act of 2017 ("TCJA"), Congress enhanced the ability of property owners to take deductions for certain qualifying property expenditures. Various improvements to non-residential property, as well as furnishings for "lodging" properties, were newly covered under TCJA (these tax benefits are beyond the scope of this book, and easily could change before this copy gathers much dust).[43] It is important to remember that most near-term depreciation benefits come at the cost of future depreciation-recapture taxes, especially if you are unable to adequately exchange §1245 property. For landlords in lower tax brackets, there may not be much advantage to trading income tax today for recapture tax tomorrow. As always, be sure to consult with your tax professional when considering the impact of claiming depreciation deductions for real or tangible property.

POLITICS AND POLICY

Much like §1031 exchanges, capital-gains taxation occasionally resurfaces in the media as a topic for "reform". Critics of the step-up in basis argue that the incentive to retain assets late in life results in money being "locked out" of other sectors of the economy. They also suggest that this long-standing tax policy primarily benefits wealthier taxpayers, who are in a better position than less affluent taxpayers to pass property on at death. In reality, continued ownership by a retired couple of successive real estate investments is hardly locking away dollars from the U.S. economy. Rather, the step-up rule is an easy target for populist vote-seekers who seem to forget how much rental property is owned by working families, not merely the uber-rich.

While we are confident that §1031 exchanges, depreciation deductions and the step-up rule will all remain more-or-less intact, it is important to be vigilant about Congress chipping away at the edges of these rare advantages in the tax code.

CHAPTER 7

Deeper in the Weeds:
A Summary of Select Challenges in §1031 Exchanges

CONDEMNATION/INVOLUNTARY CONVERSION

IRC §1031 has a close cousin—§1033. We certainly hope you will not need to rely on §1033, because it typically means that a government entity has taken your real estate, or there has been some other involuntary conversion of your property. The situations that trigger §1033 include:

- Eminent domain actions
- Destruction by forces out of your control
- Theft
- Seizure by law enforcement

Unlike the broad allowance for replacement property under §1031, §1033 requires that the new property be functionally similar and of the same use as the converted property (condemned business or investment property is subject to the wider *like-kind* standard).

The timelines under §1033 are different, too. You have two or three years to close on a replacement property, depending on the nature of the conversion. As with many IRS rules, there are specific notice requirements that you (or your accountant) must follow.

Also, §1033 does not require the use of a Qualified Intermediary, but rather a neutral third party. Nevertheless, we recommend that you use a QI anyway, to minimize the risk of negligent commingling or misappropriation.

Of course, deferring capital-gains tax after a condemnation or involuntary conversion is only necessary if the episode produced an otherwise taxable gain, such as an insurance payout. Be sure to talk with a qualified tax professional if you think you may qualify for a §1033 exchange. The principles set forth in this book for choosing replacement properties would apply equally to a §1033 situation.

SELLER FINANCING/INSTALLMENT SALES

Suppose you sell your unencumbered relinquished property, but want to act as the "bank" in financing part of the buyer's purchase price. If you pay yourself (more accurately, pay into escrow) the amount of the purchase loan in exchange for the note, such that the total purchase price (net of transaction costs) is paid to the QI account, then you can reinvest all of the proceeds into a replacement property and properly defer your capital-gains taxes.* Arrangements like these—legitimate seller financing to produce interest income—can be structured well within §1031 rules. It may even be possible to borrow money to fund the note, or to assign the note to the seller of the replacement property as consideration for the purchase.

Alternatively, an installment sale is an arrangement whereby you receive at least one payment from the buyer after the tax year of the sale. If you realize a gain on an installment sale, you

---

* Loan principal payments are return-of-capital and interest is taxable income.

may be able to report part of your gain when you receive each payment. This method of reporting gain is called the "installment method". You cannot use the installment method to report a loss, but you can choose to forego this method and report all of your gain in the year of sale.[44]

As noted earlier, deferring recognition of gain under the installment method may have limited benefit if most of your gain derives from depreciation recapture, which is entirely taxable in the year of sale.

Seller financing may enter a gray area when ostensible exchangers rely on both exchange rules and installment rules to delay recognition of gain under state and federal tax laws. As noted in Chapter V, the California Franchise Tax Board ("FTB") (and likely other states to follow) published a Notice in 2019 announcing its intent to deter the practice of combining a supposed §1031 exchange with a supposed §453 installment sale[45]:

> *FTB is aware of arrangements in which a taxpayer or QI attempts to convert proceeds from a failed like-kind exchange, or the unreinvested portion of proceeds from a partial like-kind exchange, into an installment payment structure such as an installment note or similar arrangement in which payments are to be paid out over two or more years (the "Transaction"). These arrangements do not allow for a deferral of gain recognition under Internal Revenue Code ("IRC") sections 453 and 1031 since, among other reasons, these sections and the federal doctrine of constructive receipt do not support such a deferral of gain recognition.*

The Notice also requires QIs to withhold taxes on these transactions (3.33% of the sales price or an alternative withholding calculation based on the gain required to be recognized from the sale) and imposes a penalty on QIs who fail to comply.

The rules and procedures around seller financing, installment sales and "failed exchanges" are complicated. You should not attempt to navigate these waters without an experienced tax professional.

PARTNERSHIP AND LLC ISSUES

Years ago, one of us (Richard) attended a multi-hour continuing-education course dealing extensively with the issue of partnerships in §1031 exchanges. It is impossible to summarize this topic effectively in a couple pages, but here we go.

Every day in the United States, the members of some partnership or LLC reach a point of irreconcilable differences. Sometimes these entities own real estate, and some of those entities require a §1031 exchange so that one or more of the partners may defer their taxes if the property must be sold. If only one partner wants out, and the other owners are not willing or able to cash out his/her interest, selling the partnership's property may be unavoidable. And to the extent that the remaining partners are able to buy out a single partner/member without needing to sell a property, the timing of that transaction relative to a previous or future §1031 exchange may have adverse tax consequences.

When partners want out of a partnership or LLC conducting a §1031 exchange, there are two general categories of situations. In either case, as the amount of time between the dissolution and the property sale gets closer, it is more likely that the IRS will disallow an exchange:

- Partial or full liquidation of the entity <u>before</u> the exchange
- Partial or full liquidation of the entity <u>after</u> the exchange

Not to be confused with "swap until you drop" from Chapter VI, tax attorneys use a similar expression, "drop and swap", meaning leaving or dissolving a partnership immediately before an exchange. This approach is generally disfavored, as the parties to the exchange technically are new owners and did not hold the relinquished property long enough to be considered "held for productive use in a trade or business or for investment".

When a partnership interest is "dropped" sometime *after* an exchange, continuity of ownership arguably has been maintained before and through the transaction. Practitioners have differing opinions on how long the entity should wait after the exchange to make changes to the partnership/LLC ownership structure, as the intent to hold for investment applies to both the relinquished and replacement properties. Therefore, an immediate dissolution, depending on the circumstances, could be highly problematic. Also relevant in post-exchange distributions is whether the distribution itself is tax-free, as is often the case with trusts, partnerships and LLCs, but not with other entities.[46]

Again, timing is very important in establishing "use... for investment". In a 2001 report, Congress's Joint Committee on Taxation noted a significant lack of certainty as to whether a transfer from a partnership is permissible for §1031 purposes shortly before or after an exchange.[47] When Congress itself is not sure about the state of the law, this creates an atmosphere for courts, taxing agencies, attorneys and CPAs to interpret rules differently.

Some of the techniques employed to release partners/members from entities that own real estate, assuming adequate time has passed before or after a §1031 exchange, include:
- Distributing undivided interests in the real estate
- Converting the partnership to TIC interests
- Refinancing the property to generate sufficient capital to buy out a departing partner/member
- Dividing the partnership into separate entities

Note that the IRS monitors these transactions—there are two "flagging" questions on the IRS partnership tax return (Form 1065) related to the distribution of real estate owned by the entity.[48] Generally more accepted is the formation, rather than dissolution, of a grantor trust or single-purpose LLC, and possibly a partnership entity, by the owners of a property sometime after an exchange.[49]

Do not even consider making changes to your partnership, LLC or other entity, especially in the context of a §1031 exchange, without first consulting a qualified tax professional.

RELATED-PARTY TRANSACTIONS

IRC §1031(f) provides that a tax-deferred exchange will be disallowed if the exchanger trades property with a "related property", and either party sells one of the exchange properties within two years. The purpose behind the rule is to prevent people from engaging in sham property swaps to shift their cost basis and then cashing out of properties with much lower tax consequences.

Under Revenue Ruling 2002-83, you generally cannot purchase your replacement property from a related party, regardless of the two-year holding period, unless the related party also conducts a §1031 exchange involving the same property. However, you likely can sell your relinquished property to a related party, provided you purchase your replacement property from a legitimate third party.[50] This is admittedly an over-simplification of numerous codes, regulations and court cases. Application of the law may depend on which Circuit Court of Appeals has jurisdiction over your state.

Be careful about being too clever in these situations. Even if you involve additional entities or extra steps in a series of transactions that achieve the same result as a direct related-party exchange, the IRS will apply an "economic substance" test and likely disallow the non-recognition of gain.[51]

For a §1031 exchange, the term "related party" includes your:[52]
- Full or half-siblings
- Spouse
- Ancestors
- Descendants
- Business entity of which you own, directly or indirectly, at least 50%

It is possible to have no ulterior motive in transacting with a related party, and still end up having your exchange disallowed. If you are considering buying or selling an exchange property with a relative or business entity of which you own an interest, immediately consult with an experienced tax professional.

PURCHASING FROM FOREIGN PARTIES

If you buy your replacement property from a foreign person or entity owned by foreign persons, the Foreign Investment in Real Property Tax Act of 1980 ("FIRPTA") may apply to your purchase. A nonresident alien individual is the clearest example of a foreign person, but there are several others.

FIRPTA is a federal tax law that imposes U.S. income tax on foreign persons selling U.S. real estate. Under FIRPTA, if you buy real estate from a foreign person, you may be required to withhold 15% of the amount realized from the sale.[53]

Within 20 days of the sale, you are required to file Form 8288 with the IRS and submit the 15% withholding. In essence, you are forced to pre-pay the foreign person's tax and then hope to be paid back from the IRS. It is possible to obtain an exemption to this requirement, but you still must submit the withholding while waiting for approval.

If you find yourself in this situation, you will need to replace the withholding amount with cash from outside your exchange—unless your exemption is granted and the IRS returns the funds to the QI before you need the money to close the transaction, which is not likely. Therefore, you should count on needing to pay for the 15% withholding with outside funds.*

DEVELOPMENT/CONSTRUCTION

This book is for people seeking to simplify their lives, not looking to enter into the most complex version of an exchange: improving a property during the exchange holding period (i.e., before you own it). But we would be remiss if we did not acknowledge what is often called a "build to suit" exchange.

---

* In a very limited exception, there is no withholding in a simultaneous exchange with a foreign person involving no boot. Investment Property Exchange Services, Inc., *1031 Exchange Topics*. 2019.

These are the basic steps in the process:[54]

1. You sell your relinquished property in a typical §1031 exchange, with the proceeds held by a QI.

2. You identify a property that you want to develop or improve.

3. Your QI agrees to act as an Exchange Accommodation Titleholder ("EAT") and purchases the property via a special-purpose vehicle (usually an LLC).

4. If there is a lender for the property (which could be yourself, the QI or a bank), the EAT typically will be a party to a non-recourse loan, which you must guarantee. There are multiple agreements in place to cover the entire arrangement, including the future assignment of the property or LLC and the loan.

5. During the maximum 180-day exchange period, you typically oversee the construction project, directing the EAT to make payments to contractors as needed.

6. If the fair market value of the newly improved property does not quite equal or exceed the value of your relinquished property by the time you take title, the difference will be "boot" and trigger recognition of gain.

7. You will rightfully pay your QI much more for this type of transaction, as there is considerably more work and liability for the QI than a standard forward exchange.

If this legal and procedural minefield sounds compelling, there are numerous resources with information on this subject, including top Qualified Intermediaries who specialize in complex exchange transactions.

REVERSE EXCHANGES

In Revenue Procedure 2000-37, the IRS provided "safe harbor" guidance for conducting a reverse exchange. This allows you to secure your replacement property before your sell your relinquished property. Though far less common than a forward exchange, this strategy is very handy for people who have stumbled on a great opportunity that may not remain available after they sell the investment property they already own.

Like the other topics in this chapter, there are many subtle variations on reverse exchanges, with more than one way to conduct the process within the rules. A typical transaction may go something like this:[55]

1. In contemplation of selling a property you already own, you decide to buy its replacement in advance.

2. Your QI agrees to act as an Exchange Accommodation Titleholder ("EAT") and purchases the property via a special-purpose vehicle (usually an LLC).

3. Similar to a build-to-suit exchange, you, the QI or a bank may lend the funds necessary to acquire the property.

4. You and the EAT enter into an NNN lease, so that you assume some responsibility for the property while the EAT retains title and is treated as the beneficial owner during the exchange period (sometimes called the "parking period").

5. Upon closing the above purchase, you have 45 days to identify which property you plan to sell, and have 180 days to complete the sale.

6. When the relinquished-property sale closes, you use the proceeds to formally acquire the replacement property for the EAT. The QI uses the proceeds from the sale to pay down the loan on the replacement property.

In the nine westernmost U.S. states (within the Ninth Circuit Tax Court), a case decided in 2016 provides guidance for conducting a "non-safe-harbor exchange". Specifically, this case (*Estate of George H. Bartell v. Commissioner*) allows for a longer exchange period than 180 days, and does not require that the EAT bear any burdens of ownership—provided that the EAT is not deemed to be acting as an agent of the exchanger.[56]

Before attempting to conduct a reverse exchange, be sure to consult with both an experienced QI (preferably an active member of the Federation of Exchange Accommodators) and a qualified tax professional.

PART 3

FINDING A SUITABLE SOLUTION

This page intentionally left blank

CHAPTER 8

Transition from Active Ownership
DSTs, TICs and Single-Tenant Triple-Net-Lease Properties

The premise of the remainder of this book is that you are strongly considering selling one or more of your rental properties and conducting a §1031 exchange. We assume you are motivated to pursue this transaction for these primary reasons:
- Improve the quality of your life
- Maximize the tax benefits of continued real estate ownership
- Potentially increase your real estate income

Furthermore, we assume you are interested in certain benefits from your replacement property, which may include:
- Hassle-free financing
- Institutional asset management
- Diversification across geography, tenants and sectors

Depending on the type of program you invest in, transitioning to passive ownership means releasing authority over some key elements, including:
- Day-to-day property management
- Obtaining and releasing tenants
- Refinancing

- Determining when to list a property for sale
- Paying others to source, supervise and sell the real estate

For people who really love rolling up their sleeves and operating their own properties, giving up control and paying sponsor fees may not be worth the other benefits listed above. Yet for many passive investors, freedom from management is a selling point, not a catch.

In this chapter, we will address the three most common forms of passive real estate programs—namely DSTs, TICs and single-tenant NNN-lease properties—with DSTs requiring the least involvement from investors.

DELAWARE STATUTORY TRUSTS ("DSTs")

In 2004, the IRS Office of the Associate Chief Counsel for Pass-throughs and Special Industries wrote a document known as a Revenue Ruling, which sets forth official agency policy guidelines for specific tax situations. In this case, the Ruling was numbered 2004-86, and whether its authors were aware at the time, this visionary document sparked what is now a $7 billion-per-year "niche" industry.[‡]

The Ruling addressed two questions:[57]

1. How is a Delaware Statutory Trust treated for federal income tax purposes, and
2. May a taxpayer exchange real property for a DST interest in a §1031 exchange?

In a nutshell, the IRS answered these questions by stating that 1) a DST will be treated as a trust and a separate entity from its beneficial owners, and 2) yes, an investment in a real estate-owning DST will qualify for a §1031 exchange, if the trust meets all of the requirements set forth in Chapter V above. In case you skipped that part, the IRS essentially requires that a DST program invest only in real estate, with one lease, one loan, one round of investors, one portfolio, all potential net income distributed to investors and no expenditures for major improvements. Due to the limited powers and privileges afforded to beneficial owners of DSTs under Delaware law, investors receive the dual benefit of attributed ownership of the underlying property and protection from creditors under the trust.

DST Structure

It is no exaggeration to say that Revenue Ruling 2004-86 revolutionized the world of §1031 exchanges. By blessing the framework of a qualified DST program, the IRS allowed for attributes that did not exist previously in passive §1031 investments:[58]

- **Over one hundred investors in one program,** rather than the limit of 35 under a TIC structure (see next section)
- Opportunity to **invest in a larger portfolio** of real estate than TICs
- **Only one borrower**—the DST—rather than all investors being a party to the loan
- Virtual real estate **ownership without being on title**
- Ability of the DST manager to **make decisions without a unanimous vote** of investors, an often difficult requirement for TIC programs

To be clear, a Revenue Ruling is not an act of Congress nor even an official IRS regulation. There is no guarantee that a DST offering is entirely compliant with §1031 regulations simply because it follows the guidelines set forth in Rev. Ruling 2004-86. Nevertheless, after 15 years (as of the writing of this book) and several hundred programs later, it appears that the real estate industry, the IRS, the broker-dealer community and lenders have all become comfortable with the standard template for §1031-driven DST offerings. This can be summarized as follows:

1. A real estate firm—known as a "Sponsor"—secures one or more properties for acquisition under a single DST ownership structure.
2. The Sponsor may also obtain financing from a bank,

insurance company or other lending institution to purchase the property. If there is a loan, the typical loan-to-value ("leverage") is 45%-55%.

3. The Sponsor uses affiliated entities to manage the trust, often master-lease the property(ies) and provide the initial seed capital.

4. Once the financing and purchase agreement(s) are in place, the Sponsor creates a business plan and private placement memorandum ("PPM") for the DST offering. The latter is completed in coordination with a "managing broker-dealer", who is tasked with forming a syndicate of other securities broker-dealers to raise capital primarily from §1031 investors.

5. Around the time that the DST takes title to the underlying property(ies), the managing broker-dealer typically obtains a due-diligence report from a third-party analyst firm, and then distributes the report and the PPM to potential members of the syndicate.

6. A small network of independent broker-dealers who offer "alternative" investments will approve the new offering for sale by their registered firms. Nationwide, a number of firms legitimately specialize in real estate securities programs for §1031 exchanges.

7. At this point, the Sponsor has effectively sold the properties to the DST in exchange for initial beneficial interests. The price of the property is marked up to reflect all of the transactional expenses incurred by the Sponsor, as well as some amount of profit.

8. As investors join the DST, they replace the Sponsor's original interests, thereby gradually reducing the Sponsor's ownership over the offering period.

9. An investor's percentage ownership (an "undivided beneficial interest" in the underlying properties) is based on his

or her equity investment divided by the total equity interests sold in the offering, typically known as the "Offering Amount". If there is a loan on the portfolio, investors also are allocated the same percentage interest in the total debt, for exchange purposes, as their equity interest.

10. As in any §1031 exchange, the funds for a DST investment come from the Qualified Intermediary, who holds the sales proceeds from the relinquished property. Unlike traditional real estate, a §1031 DST investment often is completed before the investor's 45-day identification period expires.

11. When all of the original equity in a DST program has been resold to new investors, the offering is closed, and no new interests in the DST can be sold. This process can take anywhere from a few weeks to a few months, depending on the Sponsor and the size of the offering.

12. Net of the reserves, operating expenses, debt service and fees, all proceeds from the underlying DST properties are distributed to investors on a monthly or quarterly basis. In many DST programs, there is a master-lease structure that includes a base rent and additional rent, resulting in a potential income stream for investors.

13. Many DST programs also rely on "interest only" loans that do not amortize for five to seven years. Sponsors strive to sell the property at the end of the interest-only period, in order to avoid a decrease in distributions. However, there is no guarantee that a property will be sold under any time frame, and the PPMs typically illustrate a *pro forma* that extends for 10 years.

14. The DST manager controls all aspects of the property. Between the offering period and liquidation, a DST investor should have virtually no participation in the program, other than receiving the potential distributions into his or her bank account or reading quarterly reports. Although

performance is not guaranteed, if the property's performance follows the numbers projected in the PPM, the investors should experience an income followed by a capital gain upon sale—assuming there has been some appreciation of the property beyond the offering price.

15. Along the way, each DST investor will be allocated his/her share of the property's depreciation. When the property is sold, that depreciation will impact his/her cost basis, which carried over from the relinquished property during the §1031 exchange that triggered the investment.

16. Upon sale of the portfolio, a DST investor has three options:
    • Take the cash and pay any outstanding federal and state capital-gains taxes; or
    • Conduct another §1031 exchange by buying his/her own rental property; or
    • Do what most DST investors do: §1031 exchange into another DST program.

The following page contains a diagram of a sample DST with one apartment community.

DST Investment Process

If you have invested in a non-traded REIT, syndicated limited partnership or energy program, investing in a DST will seem familiar. After reading the PPM and discussing options with your advisors and family, you will complete a Purchaser Questionnaire and Subscription Agreement (along with any new account forms and disclosures that your broker-dealer requires). The typical program has a $100,000 investment minimum, which means you can create a portfolio of DSTs in most situations. Alternatively, if you are purchasing a single rental property in a §1031 exchange, but the purchase price is less than the sales price of your relinquished property, a DST can be a good solution for investing what would otherwise be taxable boot.

Most §1031 DST investors today owned their relinquished property in a trust or LLC, and therefore will hold their DST

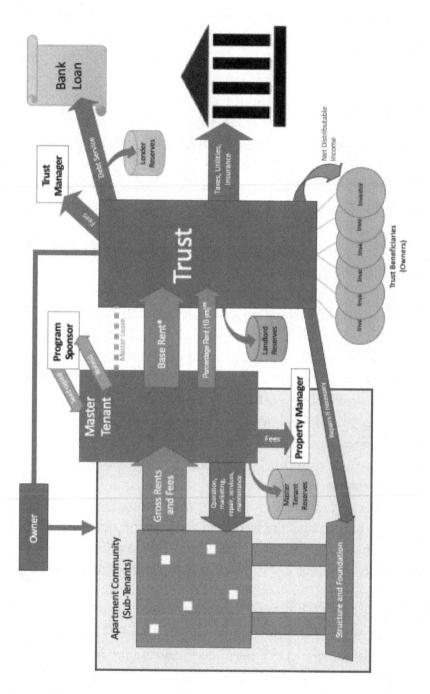

Figure 3. Diagram of parties and affiliated entities in a hypothetical DST program.

interests in the same entity. If you purchase a DST interest in your name as an individual, but later create a trust, you can easily change the registration of your DST ownership. If you pass away while owning a DST—for example, in the name of your living trust—your trust will continue receiving payments, uninterrupted, until the DST portfolio is sold. Your heirs then have the option to simply cash out or conduct another §1031 exchange.

In the unlikely event that a DST program were to somehow violate the restrictions set forth in Rev. Ruling 2004-86 (e.g., a lender bankruptcy requiring refinancing), or the lease provisions were somehow interpreted to constitute a partnership arrangement, or some catastrophic event triggered a loan default, the typical DST agreement includes a provision whereby the DST converts to a "springing" LLC, with each beneficial owner becoming a *pro rata* LLC shareholder. Under current law, a liquidation of assets under this scenario would preclude the opportunity to conduct another §1031 exchange. Notwithstanding these remote possibilities, the investment experience for most DST owners is rather uneventful: an initial purchase in the context of an exchange, followed by years of continuous potential distributions, capped finally with a distribution of proceeds, either directly to the investor or to his/her designated qualified intermediary.

DST Taxation

DST investing affords the opportunity to upgrade from a single property to fractional interests in multiple properties across several states. This benefit is further multiplied by the ability to invest in perhaps two or three DST programs as part of one §1031 exchange.

Many of the most popular states for DST properties—particularly Texas and Florida—do not impose a state tax on rental income. This is a welcome surprise for investors in states like California and Oregon. But if your DST portfolio includes a property located in an income-tax state, it will be necessary for your tax professional to file a separate state income tax return in that jurisdiction(s).

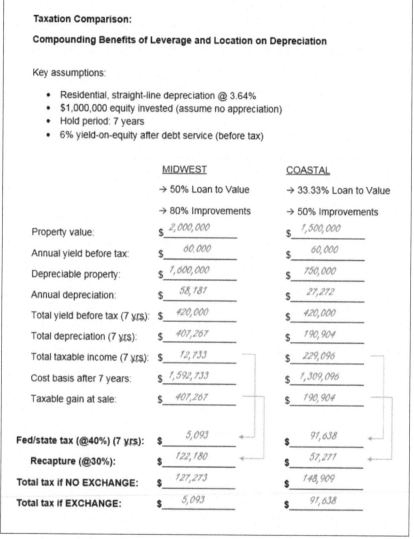

Taxation Comparison:

Compounding Benefits of Leverage and Location on Depreciation

Key assumptions:

- Residential, straight-line depreciation @ 3.64%
- $1,000,000 equity invested (assume no appreciation)
- Hold period: 7 years
- 6% yield-on-equity after debt service (before tax)

	MIDWEST	COASTAL
	→ 50% Loan to Value	→ 33.33% Loan to Value
	→ 80% Improvements	→ 50% Improvements
Property value:	$ 2,000,000	$ 1,500,000
Annual yield before tax:	$ 60,000	$ 60,000
Depreciable property:	$ 1,600,000	$ 750,000
Annual depreciation:	$ 58,181	$ 27,272
Total yield before tax (7 yrs):	$ 420,000	$ 420,000
Total depreciation (7 yrs):	$ 407,267	$ 190,904
Total taxable income (7 yrs):	$ 12,733	$ 229,096
Cost basis after 7 years:	$ 1,592,733	$ 1,309,096
Taxable gain at sale:	$ 407,267	$ 190,904
Fed/state tax (@40%) (7 yrs):	$ 5,093	$ 91,638
Recapture (@30%):	$ 122,180	$ 57,271
Total tax if NO EXCHANGE:	$ 127,273	$ 148,909
Total tax if EXCHANGE:	$ 5,093	$ 91,638

Table 8.

Each DST manager provides an annual investor letter to each beneficial owner. The report (for completing Schedule E) breaks down the investor's *pro rata* share of net income, and includes all information necessary for your tax professional to file all required tax returns. Unlike a Schedule K-1, which is used to report income/losses from a partnership, the Schedule E is for reporting income and expenses for rental income. This difference reflects the fact that a DST investment is treated more like a direct-ownership interest and less like a partnership interest, a key distinction in qualifying for a §1031 exchange.

Upon investing in a leveraged DST program in the Midwest or Southeast, you may notice that little or none of your distributions are subject to federal taxes. This is likely because of the combined effect of two common DST attributes: 1) an increase in the ratio of depreciable improvements to land, due to the relatively lower land values between the coasts, and 2) the mathematical effect of acquiring more depreciable real estate per dollar, through the use of debt financing (typically around 50% LTV).

In the worksheet above, excerpted from the authors' CPA continuing education course, we compare scenarios to see how higher leverage and depreciable improvements can greatly reduce taxes. By "Coastal", we mean a property located in a market like Los Angeles, Silicon Valley, Seattle, or New York City. In markets like these, the underlying land is often worth as much or more than the improvements, resulting in a low depreciation ratio.

While every DST investment program is different, this table illustrates how a hypothetical property with lower relative land value and slightly higher leverage, producing the same yield, can result in significantly lower taxes—especially if the investor conducts another §1031 exchange. Over seven years, the Coastal 33% LTV property triggers over $85,500 more tax than the Midwest 50% LTV property, a difference of 8.55% on a $1 million equity investment. That is the equivalent of adding 1.2% per year to the yield.

DST Industry Snapshot[59]

As of 2019, the seven most common states for DST properties are Texas, Florida, Georgia, Illinois, Tennessee, North Carolina and Virginia. It is no coincidence that most of these states are both taxpayer friendly and landlord friendly. Washington, another state with no income tax and a thriving economy, also hosts a handful of offerings. Overall, 42 states have seen DST programs in the last couple years.

The most popular asset type among DSTs is multifamily (large apartment communities), representing half of all DST offerings. Retail is the second-most popular at 10%-15%.[‡] Beyond that, investing evens out among multiple categories, including office, medical, self-storage, industrial and student housing. Over the course of a year, virtually all types of real estate can be found in DST programs. Regardless of the number of actual tenants/residents in a DST property, there is typically one master lease with the DST, under which the occupants are sub-tenants.

Roughly 35 DST sponsors will offer nearly 100 programs over a given year. As in many industries, the top eight sponsors typically represent 75% of all sales. That leaves over two-dozen sponsors scrapping for a quarter of the business. Unfortunately, this imbalance inevitably leads to a few failed firms, making **track record, commitment to the space** and **financial strength** key differentiators for choosing prospective DST investments.

Over $3.5 billion in equity and over $7 billion in total capital is now invested in passive §1031 programs annually. For comparison, in 2003—the year before the IRS recognized DST programs as viable replacement real estate—investors placed only $756 million of equity into such programs (all of these were TICs, discussed below).[‡]

Due to DSTs supplanting TICs as the preferred passive §1031 program, the average deal size (equity offering amount) has grown from under $11 million in 2007 to nearly $29 million in 2019.[‡] More and more offerings include multi-property portfolios, sometimes representing multiple states within one program.

You may be thinking, "This is all great, but how much do these DSTs pay?" Some programs are designed for pure appreciation (no income), while other DSTs invest in Class-B properties at 8+% cap rates. But the majority of §1031 DST programs, currently, project first-year cash distributions ranging from 4% to 6%. We will touch on *pro forma* financial projections and assumptions in the next chapter.

TENANT-IN-COMMON INTERESTS ("TICs")

The term "tenant in common" goes back to British property law, and refers to multiple people owning undivided interests in a piece of real estate. Unlike "joint tenants with right of survivorship", if a tenant-in-common dies, his interest passes to his estate rather than to the other owners. Most spouses co-own their property with rights of survivorship in the United States, while TIC ownership is prevalent among all other types of multi-owner arrangements.

Real estate sponsors have been structuring investment programs as TICs for a few decades. By the late 1990s, a handful of sponsors were packaging and syndicating TICs as replacement properties for §1031 exchanges. Early pioneers included Passco, formed in Orange County, California in 1998, and Inland Investments (Illinois), which established its TIC division in 2001, eventually becoming the market leader in the securitized §1031 space. Lawyers at that time relied on a patchwork of cases and IRS guidance to substantiate the qualification of these early programs as replacement properties. Seeking more certainty from the IRS, they finally received formal guidance in the form of Revenue Procedure 2002-22.[60] The key issue was how to structure a common ownership enterprise without it constituting a partnership, which cannot be the basis of a §1031 investment.

Rev. Proc. 2002-22 set forth guidelines for §1031-qualified TIC programs, including the following important provisions:
- Co-ownership may not resemble an entity.
- The co-owners must retain the right to approve:
  » hiring of any manager

» disposition of the property

» creation or modification of a blanket lien

- Any sale, lease, or re-lease of a portion or all of the property, any negotiation or renegotiation of indebtedness secured by a blanket lien, the hiring of any manager, or the negotiation of any management contract (or any extension or renewal of such contract) must be by unanimous approval of the co-owners.

- Each co-owner must have the rights to transfer, partition and encumber the co-owner's undivided interest in the property without the agreement or approval of any person.*

- If the property is sold, any debt secured by a blanket lien must be satisfied and the remaining sales proceeds must be distributed to the co-owners.

- Each co-owner must share in all revenues generated by the property and all costs associated with the property in proportion to the co-owner's undivided interest in the property, as well as any indebtedness.

- Any payment to the sponsor for the acquisition of the co-ownership interest must reflect the fair market value and may not depend, in whole or in part, on the income or profits derived by any person from the property.

Based on the certainty these guidelines provided, the TIC industry grew rapidly after 2002, with the Tenant-in-Common Association

---

* However, restrictions on the right to transfer, partition, or encumber interests in the property that are required by a lender and that are consistent with customary commercial lending practices are not prohibited. Moreover, the co-owners, the sponsor, or the lessee may have a right of first offer (the right to have the first opportunity to offer to purchase the co-ownership interest) with respect to any co-owner's exercise of the right to transfer the co-ownership interest in the property. In addition, a co-owner may agree to offer the co-ownership interest for sale to the other co-owners, the sponsor, or the lessee at fair market value (determined as of the time the partition right is exercised) before exercising any right to partition.

** TICA later evolved into the Alternative & Direct Investment Securities Association (ADISA), a leading trade organization for sponsors and distributors of securitized real estate and other "alternative" investments.

("TICA")** forming in 2003 to establish uniform program standards, and with multiple Sponsors joining the field. At its peak in 2006, over $3.5 billion of §1031 equity flowed into TIC programs.

Yet there were multiple challenges to the TIC structure. First, 35 investors was a silly and arbitrary limit, forcing offerings to remain small. Secondly, each investor had to execute loan documents and deeds, creating a 37-party contractual cluster on every program (seller, bank and 35 investors). Thirdly, the IRS-mandated voting require- ment allowed single investors, on occasion, to sabotage the collective decisions of the remaining owners, particularly with respect to selling.

With the advent of DSTs in 2004, §1031 sponsors gravi- tated toward the new structure after the Great Recession. Under heightened scrutiny by regulators, greater attention by selling firms, and overall awareness from Internet searches and social media, sponsors also lowered their fees post-recession. Some of the smaller TIC sponsors did not survive the last real estate cycle and ensuing regulatory changes, but today's top sponsors are arguably stronger and better prepared for any future disruptions in the real estate market.

We continue to see passive §1031 TIC programs, as they may be more appropriate for niche strategies involving significant capital improvements or properties where master leases are not practical. Regardless of whether a §1031 program is structured as a DST or a TIC, the same basic real estate investment principles and risks apply, which we address in the next chapter.

SINGLE-TENANT, TRIPLE-NET-LEASE PROPERTIES

The first part of the above heading is straightforward—a single tenant means there is only one tenant in the building. Common examples include:

- Fast-food restaurants
- Big-box retail stores

- Banks
- Warehouses

In the residential world, a single-tenant property would be a detached home as opposed to an apartment complex. In any of these examples, you are dealing typically with one structure and one tenant, which has the virtue of a very simple relationship.

The second part of the above heading—Triple Net Lease—may be less intuitive. The term "triple net" comes from the third and fourth broad categories of net leases (distinct from *gross* leases, which are based on the revenues of the tenant), derived from the general types of expenses for which the tenant is responsible:

Single Net Lease
- Tenant pays base rent + property taxes
- Landlord pays all other operating expenses

Double Net Lease (NN)
- Tenant pays base rent + property taxes + property insurance
- Landlord pays all other operating expenses

Triple Net Lease (NNN)
- Tenant pays base rent + property taxes + property insurance + maintenance
- Landlord maintains the structural integrity of the building

Absolute Triple Net Lease (Bond Lease)
- Tenant is responsible for everything

Hereinafter, we will refer to single-tenant, triple-net-lease properties as "ST-NNNs".

Real estate brokers often market ST-NNNs as passive §1031 replacement properties with the following potential benefits:
- Long-term leases
- Rental income you can forecast to the penny
- Hassle-free ownership

- Sometimes "credit rated" tenants, meaning a parent company with deep pockets in the event of a default

It is easy to understand the appeal of ST-NNNs. One example of a scenario may go something like this:

- You purchase a stand-alone drive-through Taco World sitting in the middle of a mall parking lot for $1.667 million, and lease it back to a new or existing franchisee at a 6% cap rate.
- This type of structure is usually 3,000-4,000 square feet, on roughly one-half acre of land.
- Although the franchisee is not an investment-grade tenant, you are banking on the strength and durability of the Taco World brand.
- Unless you can obtain a corporate-backed ground lease from the Taco World parent company, in most cases you are looking to the franchisee for creditworthiness in a 10-year NNN lease with annual rent bumps of, say, 2%.
- Once the lease is signed, you rest easy, knowing that demand for Taco World will continue to drive stable, predictable income into your bank account for years to come.

Now suppose eight years goes by. The mall where the Taco World sits has closed. Although you have maintained your property, the parking lot asphalt surrounding the restaurant is disintegrating. What's more, shifts in eating habits have impacted demand for Taco World's beef, lard and dairy-based menu. The tenants inform you that they are going out of business, but will agree to pay six of the remaining 24 months' rent if you agree not to sue them. Otherwise they will be forced to file bankruptcy.

After settling, you now have an empty Taco World that is equipped for only one type of tenant: a fast-food restaurant. You decide to sell, recognizing that at least you had eight years of solid rental income. One of your broker friends mentions that cap rates on fast-food restaurants are only 100 basis points higher than eight years ago, so you should not have to worry about the sale price. You neglect to mention that your property is vacant, and that $0.00 net income divided by a cap rate of 7.0% is $0.00. Unless a buyer has a tenant in hand, or intends to occupy the property, you likely will need to secure another tenant for your former Taco World building (adjacent to the closed mall) before having any hope of selling.

Now let us suppose that your tenants remained in business and continued paying the rent. And let us imagine that they agreed to a 10-year extension, under the same exact rent terms, at the end of their lease. Assuming the revenue at purchase was $100,000, then an annual 2% rent bump after 10 years would equate to $121,900. That sounds great, but if inflation has increased by more than 2% per year, your $121,900 annual income is worth less than when you started.

You decide to sell, hoping the renewed lease will be attractive to a prospective buyer. Because cap rates on fast-food restaurants next to malls have increased to 7.0%, your sales price (if you are lucky) is now $121,900 ÷ 0.07 = $1.741 million. After sales costs, you will have sold the property for less than you paid for it.

ST-NNN properties come with four important related risks:

- Concentration risk (putting all of your eggs in one basket)
  - » One asset type
  - » One tenant
  - » One geographic market
- Tenant credit risk
  - » Your income is entirely dependent on the tenant's ability and willingness to pay rent, even when their business is bad.
- Cap rate risk
  - » In a long-term, fixed-rent agreement, you have no ability to increase revenue. If cap rates increase while revenue is flat, the property value must decrease. This result is inescapable—it is purely mathematical.
- Functional obsolescence risk
  - » As in the case of Taco World, many ST-NNN

properties cannot be adapted for re-use without significant capital expenditures.

Like any real estate investment, ST-NNN properties can be entirely appropriate for the right buyer under the right circumstances. We believe too many people purchase these deals without an adequate appreciation of their unique risks, and without an awareness of other alternatives.

To help you understand these different options for investing in passive real estate in a §1031 exchange, we have included the summary comparison grid on the next page. Values are intended to be general/typical, rather than minimum/maximum, unless otherwise indicated on the following page.

SECURITIES LAWS

In its famous decision of SEC v. W.J. Howey Co., the U.S. Supreme Court stated[61]:

An investment contract for purposes of the Securities Act means a contract, transaction or scheme whereby a person invests his money in a common enterprise and is led to expect profits solely from the efforts of the promoter or a third party.

Further, the Court said it is irrelevant whether the shares in the enterprise are evidenced by formal certificates or by nominal interests in the physical assets employed in the enterprise (in this case, land sales contracts for Florida citrus groves, which are now rapidly disappearing).

Over the years, various sponsors of passive real estate investment programs have tried to argue that their offerings are not securities. Worse, there continues to be a smattering of syndicators who pretend not to know they are violating securities laws, some of whom have gone years or decades without being investigated by FINRA or the SEC.

Let there be no doubt: any investment program in which you get paid without doing anything is a security for purposes of United

	DSTs	TICs	ST-NNNs
# of owners	100+	Maximum 35	1
# of properties	1-10	1-3	1
# of (sub) tenants	Up to 1,200	Up to 400	1
Form of investment	Fund subscription	Grant deed and TIC agreement	Grant deed and lease agreement
Party to loan?	No	Yes	Yes
Financing in place?	Yes	Yes	Typically no
LLC required by lender?	No	Yes	No
Minimum investment	$100k	$100k	Typically over $1MM
Investors approve sale?	No	Unanimous approval required for major decisions	Yes
Investment commission	Factored into property purchase price, paid indirectly by investors	Factored into property purchase price, paid indirectly by investors	Paid by seller
Acquisition fees	Factored into property purchase price, paid indirectly by investors	Factored into property purchase price, paid indirectly by investors	Not applicable
Asset management fees	Deducted from rental revenues	Deducted from rental revenues	Owners must provide their own asset management
Typical lease structure	Master lease	Master lease	NNN
Time to close after signing agreement	1 week	2 weeks	1-3 months
Liability beyond initial investment	Typically none	Limited	Full liability as sole direct owner

Table 9.

States securities laws.* (ST NNN-lease properties are not securities because, despite having delegated all responsibility to your tenant, at the end of the day you are ultimately responsible for everything that happens on a property of which you are the sole owner.) Do not let an agent without a securities license—or a program sponsor without a securities broker-dealer—try to convince you that their passive offering is somehow not a security. It is.

Because DSTs and TICs are both real estate and securities, they must be sold by someone with strong real estate knowledge and a proper securities license, typically a Series 7 (General Securities Representative) or Series 22 (Direct Participation Programs Representative registration). Although your stockbroker or maybe even your insurance agent technically could be allowed to sell you interests in a DST, it is important to work only with professionals who focus primarily on real estate securities.

Conversely, your real estate agent can neither sell, nor be paid commissions, on a DST transaction. It is simply illegal. As a result, you might not hear about DSTs from your real estate agent. Yet there are excellent real estate agents who, despite the absence of a direct incentive, regularly refer their clients to financial professionals who specialize in DSTs. Why, you might ask, would these agents point their clients to properties they cannot be paid on? As it turns out, some people will advise their clients to consider multiple options, even if some of those options become lost business. Besides, your agent will still get paid for selling your relinquished property. A smart agent will recognize the opportunity to point his/her client to the best possible §1031 solutions, even if that means not getting paid on the replacement property.

---

* When you read a typical legal opinion letter in the back of a DST PPM, you likely will see a sentence that says something like, "The Interests should not be treated as securities for purposes of Section 1031..." This may seem contradictory, but often a banana under one federal code is not a banana under another code. The important point here is that DST interests are real estate to the IRS and securities to the SEC.

From an investor perspective, there is considerable value in buying a real estate program syndicated through a network of broker-dealers. First, the sponsor is required by law—and by the selling firms—to prepare a very detailed description of the program, called a Private Placement Memorandum ("PPM"). PPMs can be up to 400 pages long. Second, a handful of third-party due diligence firms around the country provide their own independent analyses of the programs to help broker-dealers decide which deals to sell. Third, these broker-dealers conduct their own due-diligence, which typically includes visiting the sponsors' headquarters and property locations. Finally, if you have a good advisor working with you, he or she will have conducted their own analysis of both the proposed program and your individual circumstances and suitability.

If you decide to purchase a DST or TIC interest as part of a §1031 exchange, your financial professional will be required to gather far more information than your real estate agent. SEC, FINRA and federal anti-money laundering rules are triggered by the sale or solicitation of any security, whether it is a mutual fund or a private real estate program. Do not be alarmed if you are asked to provide details regarding your current investments, net worth, income, risk tolerance and investment time horizon, as well as documentation substantiating your identity, citizenship and ownership entity (LLC, trust, etc.).

Under rules of the Securities Exchange Act and other securities laws, §1031 programs are considered "private placements", meaning the programs are not required to make public filings with the SEC. With limited exceptions, private placements must be sold only to "accredited investors". There are multiple categories of accredited investors, but for individuals you can only qualify if you meet at least one of two criteria*:

• Income: $200,000 annual income per person or $300,000

---

* As of publication, Congress was considering expanding the accreditation rules.

annual income for a household

- Net worth: excluding personal residence, a total of $1 million

Despite the additional personal information necessary to comply with the above regulatory requirements, the paperwork to "subscribe" in a DST may be less onerous than any real estate transaction. Indeed, it is possible to receive and execute all related documents in one DocuSign email. The paperwork required in a TIC investment, on the other hand, typically is on par with a typical real estate purchase.

RISKS OF PASSIVE INVESTMENT PROGRAMS

Illiquidity Risk

- There is no public market for program interests.
- Once invested, there is only a very limited possibility to seek a buyer for program interests from among the other owners, and likely only at a significant discount to current value. Investors should assume their invested funds will be unavailable for the duration of the program.
- There is no specified time at which a program portfolio will be liquidated.

Control Risk

- DST investors have no control over leasing, financing, management or disposition.
- TIC investors have approval rights over critical asset management decisions, but lack of unanimity among owners can disrupt the ability of management to execute its business plan or liquidation.

Exchange Risk

- The §1031 TIC and §1031 DST industries rely on IRS guidance that dates back only to 2002 and 2004, respectively. There is not a body of case law or subsequent regulations to provide additional assurances that these programs will comply fully with IRS requirements for §1031 exchanges.

- Investors are not guaranteed an interest in the program until all agreements are signed and the exchange proceeds are transferred to the program. A purchase may be delayed and may not satisfy the timeliness requirements of IRC §1031.

Performance Risk

- There is no guarantee that investors will receive any return.
- Investment may result in loss of entire principal.
- There can be no assurance that the investment objectives described in the PPM will be achieved.
- Past performance of other properties cannot be relied upon to assess the future performance of any program.
- Distributions are not guaranteed and may be sourced from non-income items and constitute a return of capital.

Sponsor Conflicts and Fees

- A program sponsor and its affiliates are subject to conflicts of interest between their activities, roles and duties for other entities and the activities, roles and duties they have assumed on behalf of the program. Conflicts exist in allocating management time, services and functions between their current and future activities and the program. None of the arrangements or agreements between affiliated entities, including those relating to the purchase price of program properties or compensation, is the result of arm's length negotiations.
- A program sponsor and its affiliates receive substantial compensation in the form of fees for acquisition, financing, asset management, property management and disposition.
- Although a sponsor may have a long track record, the entities it creates to manage individual programs typically are *de novo* with no operating history.

Leverage Risk

- Most programs rely on leverage—an acquisition loan or similar form of indebtedness—to acquire the property. These are generally non-recourse loans, though some loans allow for "bad boy carve outs" in the event an investor commits an egregious act such as declaring bankruptcy or committing fraud.

- There can be no assurance that the disposition of the property will allow for the repayment of outstanding indebtedness.
- Leverage has the effect of amplifying any percentage gain or loss on invested equity.
- If a program does not liquidate before the interest-only period ends (typically five to seven years), loan amortization likely will result in reduced distributions to investors.

Transaction Risk

- If the program property or portfolio has not yet closed, there is a risk that the purchase may not be consummated.
- Especially in the case of new or inexperienced program sponsors, it is possible that the program could be delayed in, or fail entirely to, raise the entire equity offering amount.

Real Estate Risk

- Program investors are buying real estate, with all of the risks inherent in any real estate investment, including:
  » General acquisition, ownership and operational risks
  » Environmental, regulatory, zoning and easement issues
  » Increased competition and decreased occupancy
  » Unforeseen maintenance, repairs and capital expenditures
  » Macroeconomic changes, including interest and cap rates
  » Tenant acquisition, retention and re-leasing costs

Although significant due diligence may be performed by sponsors, lenders, third-party consultants, appraisers, broker-dealers and registered investment professionals, this does not ensure that an investment will perform as projected. There may be issues that are not discovered through due diligence prior to or following an investor's subscription in a passive §1031 program, which may cause an investor to incur losses up to the entire amount of the investment. The risks set forth herein are not exhaustive of all investment risks, and certain programs have greater or different risks than others.

The views and opinions expressed in this book are for informational purposes only as of the date of this material and are subject to change at any time. This material is not a recommendation, offer or solicitation to buy or sell any securities or engage in any particular investment strategy and should not be considered specific legal, investment or tax advice.

Please speak with your own tax and legal advisors for guidance regarding your particular situation. Because investor situations and objectives vary, this information is not intended to indicate suitability for any particular investor. Company names listed herein may have proprietary interests in their names and trademarks. Nothing herein shall be considered to be an endorsement, authorization or approval of the aforementioned companies, or the investment vehicles they may offer. Further, none of the aforementioned companies are affiliated with the authors or their affiliates in any manner. Hypothetical examples and scenarios used throughout this material are for illustration purposes only; individual results may vary.

CHAPTER 9

Knowledge is Power:
What to Ask About a §1031 Investment Program

LOCATION

We concede that a real estate investor can make money in the worst neighborhood of the worst city in the worst recession, if such heavenly stars as timing, circumstances and luck all align perfectly. In the absence of such providence, we believe that good investing starts with good locations. Below are factors in selecting suitable markets, known as Metropolitan Statistical Areas or "MSAs".

Population Trends

This may be obvious, but you generally want to buy real estate where the population is growing. A particular property could be supported by overall population growth, or by a shift from one end of town to another. According to the U.S. Census Bureau, the top ten fastest growing cities in the United States (from 2017 to 2018) are:[62]

1. Phoenix, Arizona
2. San Antonio, Texas
3. Fort Worth, Texas
4. Seattle, Washington
5. Charlotte, North Carolina
6. Austin, Texas
7. Jacksonville, Florida
8. San Diego, California
9. Denver, Colorado
10. Frisco, Texas

Unemployment / Job Growth

As of September 2019, there were 27 MSAs with an unemployment rate of 2.0% or less (with a national average of 3.3%). Without listing them all, here are the states where these cities are located:[63]

- South Carolina (6 MSAs)
- Utah (4 MSAs)
- Iowa (3 MSAs)
- North Dakota (3 MSAs)
- Colorado (3 MSAs)
- Missouri (2 MSAs)
- Maine (1 MSAs)
- Vermont (1 MSA)
- Indiana (1 MSA)
- Idaho (1 MSA)
- Texas (1 MSA)
- New Hampshire (1 MSA)

In terms of job growth, the top MSAs (as of May 2019) were:[64]

1. St. George, Utah
2. Bend, Oregon
3. Reno, Nevada
4. Nashville, Tennessee
5. Provo, Utah
6. Lake Charles, Louisiana
7. Boise City, Idaho
8. Phoenix, Arizona
9. Fort Collins, Colorado
10. Gainesville, Georgia

Rent Growth

This statistic is more specific to asset type: if you are considering buying a medical office property, you may not care about rent growth in apartments. Yet, for illustrative purposes, here are the top ten cities (population 250,000+) for apartment rental growth as of February 2019:[65]

1. Henderson, Nevada
2. Mesa, Arizona
3. Phoenix, Arizona
4. Austin, Texas
5. Las Vegas, Nevada
6. San Jose, California
7. Arlington, Texas
8. Raleigh, North Carolina
9. Charlotte, North Carolina
10. Aurora, Colorado

You may have noticed some interesting trends in this data. Notwithstanding a few small towns in New England, most of the top MSAs in these categories are in the Southeast, South and the West. Noticeably absent is California, with Silicon Valley appearing only in the rent growth category. It is no coincidence that the top states for DST programs correlate with these key statistics.

Of course, these are all backward-looking figures, and often delayed by several months. Such stats are only valuable to the extent that you believe near-term economic conditions will continue to support these MSAs' rankings. Generally this tends to be the case, but sometimes major events (e.g., dramatic oil-price drop, historic hurricane, significant employer exodus or new rent-control law) can have a sudden and material impact on a city's real estate.

At the granular level, you should also ask about supply, a major contributing factor in future rent growth. What is the current competition for this property? How much similar development is in the pipeline? What is the anticipated absorption rate for this property type in this location?

Other factors worth noting when reviewing a particular offering:
- Overall economic growth
- Pending moves by large employers (in or out)
- Vacancy rates
- Qualitative rankings on business environment or live-ability

REVENUE-GROWTH ASSUMPTIONS

If you are considering a §1031 investment program with a long-term, NNN-lease property, rental growth is a moot point.

The revenue from such properties may be nearly fixed for the entire projected life of the program.

Conversely, asset types like apartments, self-storage, senior housing, student housing, hospitality and some office and retail may have opportunities to increase revenues over time.

Landlords generally can only increase their revenue in three ways:

- Benefitting from demographic and macroeconomic forces that tilt the supply/demand balance in the owner's favor, allowing him/her to gradually raise rents as leases expire
- Generating new demand (at a higher price point) by changing or augmenting the property
- Improving tenant screening, optimizing rental rates, increasing retention and reducing average "make-ready" times between tenants

Even without revenue growth, a landlord nevertheless can increase profitability by making operational enhancements and reducing expenses. Unless a property was quite poorly managed, however, cost-cutting alone may not be a significant contributor to improved net operating income.

You should understand what is driving the revenue-growth assumptions behind any investment program. Is the sponsor relying solely on inflationary increases? Are they assuming that demographic and economic changes will naturally drive rents higher? Is there a value-enhancement element to their business plan? If these questions cannot be answered from the PPM, have your representative obtain the answers from the sponsor.

Without any reasonable rationale and data, do not accept rental-growth assumptions that exceed inflation or the projected growth rates for the MSA published by a recognized real estate data and research provider.

LEVERAGE/FINANCING

In a §1031 exchange situation, understanding leverage is critical. (Remember that you must replace the entire value of your relinquished property, including the equity and the debt.) First, you must ascertain the loan balance on your relinquished property at the time of sale—this can be found on your closing statement. Second, add your sales proceeds (equity) to the loan balance, and then divide that sum by the loan balance. The resulting quotient is the most conservative way to determine what the minimum loan-to-value ("LTV") should be in your replacement portfolio, in order to avoid "boot".

If you are looking at a range of DST options, you may have the ability to allocate between programs with different LTVs to match your relinquished LTV. Depending on preference and availability, you may choose a portfolio that results in a significant increase in leverage compared to your relinquished property. It is important to understand the ramifications.

On the positive side, using leverage—especially when there is a "spread" between the loan interest rate and the property cap rate—has the potential to amplify the return on your equity investment. Further, as previously discussed, borrowing more money to own a highly depreciable property can potentially reduce or eliminate federal income taxes on distributions.

Greater leverage also comes with greater risk, as the property could fail to produce adequate revenue to service the loan, or drop in value enough to erode investors' equity completely. In particular, properties with high leverage and flat rental growth run the risk of being clobbered by rising cap rates. This is why we prefer asset types, like apartments, with the potential for revenue growth that can outpace inflation.

Beyond the *amount* of debt, you should also be familiar with the type of debt. At a minimum, be sure to note:

- Fixed or variable rate?

» If variable, what are the interest-rate caps?
- Is there an interest-only period?
    » If so, how long?
    » How much higher will payments be upon amortization?
- Who is the lender?
- Is the loan non-recourse (typically yes)?
    » If so, what are the carve-outs, if any?
- What are the main loan covenants?

As a DST investor, your ultimate goal is to have a passive, worry-free investment experience. Being familiar with a program's basic loan terms is a great way to avoid surprises later on.

LEASE TERMS

If the underlying property in a §1031 investment program is subject to an NNN lease, then your questions should be fairly easy to answer:

- What is the lease duration?
- What is the formula for periodic rent bumps?

In a TIC that owns an office building, for example, you may have a rent roll that includes multiple tenants with varying rents, lease terms and expiration dates. The PPM should provide all of this information, but projecting future revenues from such a schedule requires assumptions on default rates and tenant retention. These assumptions should be conservative and reasonable; otherwise, the *pro forma* will produce an overly optimistic revenue projection.

For the majority of DST programs, a master lease is created for the properties, with all of the tenants technically being sub-tenants of the master tenant, an entity formed by the sponsor. Often, the terms of the master lease provide for a contractual base rent paid to the trust, with additional rent paid to the extent that revenues exceed a base-line. Both the base rent and additional rent are typically subject to a formulaic increase. This arrangement provides an economic incentive for the sponsor/manager to increase revenues, thereby aligning the

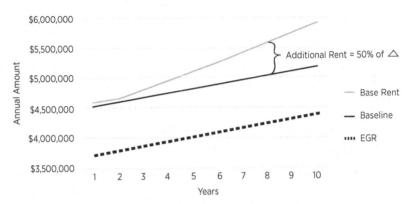

Chart 4. EGR = Effective Gross Revenue.

interests of management and investors. The following is an example of the rent terms in a DST with a master-leased apartment building.

Note that a master lease is not like an NNN lease. Each DST sponsor allocates property-related expenses differently between the trust and the master tenant. Looking back at the diagram in Figure 3, Chapter VIII, that lease requires the master tenant to cover most property management expenses, while the trust is responsible for taxes, utilities, insurance and major repairs to the structure/foundation of the apartment building. The master tenant (sponsor) bears the risk that certain property-level expenses could increase, while the trust (investors) bear the risk of unforeseen increases in property taxes or structural damage.

FEES

Securitized §1031 investment programs are more expensive than buying and operating your own real estate. This is a given. Anyone who tries to sugar-coat the fees is being disingenuous, if not shady. Yet there is considerable value being delivered for those fees, including but not limited to:

- Performing ongoing market research and data analysis
- Sourcing real estate from among thousands of listed properties around the United States

- Conducting intensive property-specific due diligence and preparing complicated financial models
- Securing optimal financing terms
- Engaging top property-management companies or, in some cases, utilizing in-house property management
- Executing value-add strategies on a massive scale
- Providing ongoing accounting and tax reporting
- Monitoring the property and the market to optimize disposition timing
- At the securities representative level, paying for client-specific services to achieve an appropriate and suitable investment solution
- Years or decades of experience from firms that often are large operators of institutional-caliber real estate portfolios

And of course, there is the incalculable value of not lifting your finger to own a fractional interest in a $50-300 million portfolio of properties.

There are four general categories of fees in any syndicated real estate investment program, beyond what an institutional buyer would incur for investing in the same property (see table below). Because of the wide variety of asset types, lease structures and program sponsors, it would be impractical to describe the myriad variations of fee structures used across all DST and TIC offerings. These numbers are estimates, subject to change, and intended to represent a range of typical fees; some Sponsors will rely more on some fees than others.

Fee Category	% of Equity
Up-front securities commissions and distribution costs (typically baked into the total offering price)	8 – 10%
Up-front acquisition and loan coordination	4 – 8%
Annual asset management/revenue participation	1 – 3%
Disposition fee	2 – 4%

Table 10.

Some of these fees/expenses are built into the total price of the offering, while others are charged on a flat percentage basis. Unlike REITs or partnership programs, DSTs do not have "preferred returns" or "waterfall" formulas when the property is liquidated.

Every PPM has a very detailed section describing all of the fees and expenses in the program.

CAP RATE ASSUMPTIONS

Suppose that a new DST property today is producing net operating income ("NOI" - before taxes, depreciation and debt service) of $5 million. The property was purchased at a cap rate of 6%, equating to a price of $83.33 million.

The sponsors have provided a pro forma that articulates an NOI increase of 20% over 10 years, for a final NOI of $6 million in the year of sale. Assume that there is a strong case for this level of income growth.

Taking the NOI at face value, what will be the value of the property in 10 years? This depends almost entirely on one assumption: the "terminal cap rate".

If we assume the terminal cap rate (literally, the cap rate at the end of the projected period, in this case 10 years) remains flat at 6.0%, then the property value will be:

$6 million ÷ 6.0% = $100 million
Final NOI   *Terminal Cap Rate*   *Sale Price*

This results in a total appreciation of $16.66 million, or 20%. All else being equal, the percentage change in NOI from purchase to sale will equal the percentage change in value.

Alas, all is not equal. Cap rates fluctuate.

Dime-store wisdom tells us that cap rates will move closely with interest rates, reflecting a simple premium for real estate over treasuries. Reality, however, has proven far more complex. To make sense of this dysfunctional relationship, economists have expressed cap rates in various algebraic terms that can be summarized as follows:

Cap Rate (R) = 10-year treasury (T) + Operating Risk (O) + Liquidity Premium (L), or R = T + O + L.

(For simplicity, this formula intentionally omits an expression of inflation and long-term cash-flow growth expectations, both of which are less impactful factors.)

Restated, R - T (the "Spread") = O + L. In other words, the spread between treasuries and cap rates is largely a function of two key variables: 1) the near-term supply/demand ratio in a given market, and 2) a premium for illiquidity.

The former is easy enough to understand—operating risk will fluctuate with changes in construction activity and demand for rental space. If improving employment rates and upward price pressures result in increased interest rates, often these same forces will drive demand for, say, apartments or warehouses. The improved economic conditions that spur interest rates can simultaneously reduce operating risk, potentially offsetting some or all of the cap-rate decompression that otherwise would occur.

Picture a girl holding a balloon while walking up a ramp. The girl represents the economy, the ramp is the 10-year treasury, and the balloon is a given cap rate. If the girl pulls down on the balloon while walking up the ramp, the balloon (cap rates) will move forward but not move up. Many of the factors that propel the girl up the ramp (better jobs, increased household formation, personal consumption) also tend to pull down on the balloon—all at the same time.

But Operating Risk is not the whole story. Our other variable in the Spread—Liquidity Premium—may be more important than Operating Risk. According to economist Dr. Peter Linneman, changes in L are a primary factor in cap-rate changes over time. L is an expression of the availability of capital to invest in real estate: when capital is pricey and scarce, the liquidity premium rises. Conversely, when money is cheap and plentiful, the liquidity premium drops.[66]

Regression analyses by Linneman suggest that, all things being equal, cap rates will rise and fall with capital market liquidity.

Furthermore, Linneman found that a 100-basis-point (1%) increase in 10-year treasury yields caused a double-digit basis-point cap-rate increase in only one sector: office. Notably, apartments proved the least sensitive to jumps in GDP growth, which drove up cap rates in other sectors.[67]

Bottom line—cap rates are highly influenced by, but do not move in lock-step with interest rates, and there is considerable variation between sectors within real estate, due to differences in construction cycles, lease duration and demand drivers. It is quite possible that cap rates in some markets could continue to compress while interest rates rise gradually over time, especially where supply is truly constrained and capital continues to chase deals.

When comparing a property's cap rate today with a 10-year projection, ask yourself or a trusted professional:

- Will interest rates be higher or lower in 10 years?
- Will the supply/demand balance for this type of property, in this location, change significantly in 10 years?
- Will the availability of capital for this type of asset change much in 10 years?

If you have definitive answers to these questions, please call us, because we certainly do not. However, we have enough sense to know if a DST sponsor is making "heroic assumptions" about future cap rates. A conservative approach would assume higher cap rates, and you should do your own cocktail-napkin math before accepting anyone else's cap rate assumptions.

SPONSOR TRACK RECORD

In the investment world, two common-sense truisms clash on a daily basis:

"The best predictor of future behavior is past behavior."
-Mark Twain

"Past performance is not a guarantee of future results."
-Every investment advertisement

Even in this book, we are careful to communicate that "Past performance of other properties cannot be relied upon to assess the future performance of any program." Clearly, the success that a sponsor had in buying, operating and selling a property in Colorado 10 years ago may not be entirely germane to a property being purchased today in Georgia. In addition to being in a different MSA, other differences include changes in interest rates, government regulations, demographic trends, macroeconomic conditions and a host of other details large and small. Moreover, personnel changes at a sponsor can be significant over a 10-year period.

And yet we still look to track record to help filter through potential programs. Marketing directors at financial services firms rely on "Old, Big and Good" as the foundation of their messaging for a reason. People take comfort in the experience, capacity and past successes of program sponsors. Admittedly, we and other professionals in our field are not immune from this sentiment. Once a sponsor has demonstrated consistent performance over multiple years and properties—even if those properties are all different—it suggests that a common level of insight, skill, talent and competence pervades the track record.

Therefore, while it should not be a determining factor, we believe it is reasonable to consider a sponsor's track record as part of your decision.

CHAPTER 10

Tying It All Together:
You Really Can Retire from Active Ownership

---

1. IMPROVE THE QUALITY OF YOUR LIFE

If you have been a landlord for a while, you probably have amassed a litany of stories about tenants, maintenance issues, plumbing emergencies or government regulations. You live with the constant threat of legal liability. Accounting, paperwork and bill-paying consume untold hours of your time. Every time the phone rings, it could be another problem with your property.

It may be time to emancipate yourself from rental ownership. You have earned a retirement from your property.

In a passive real estate program, you have:
- No advertising for new tenants
- No applicant screening and expenses
- No lease negotiations
- No tenant improvements
- No property maintenance
- No accounting or monthly expenses

- No tax or insurance bills
- No late-night emergencies
- No conversations with property managers or tenants
- No loan payments
- No listing agreements

Further, if you invest in a DST program, you have:

- No grant deed, no public record of title
- No loan application
- No reams of real estate contract documents
- No decisions to be made for leasing, financing or disposition

Indeed, your participation in your investment could be nothing more than checking for the potential electronic distribution payments into your checking account and forwarding an annual investor report to your accountant. Really.

2. POTENTIALLY INVEST IN BETTER REAL ESTATE

Most individual landlords doing a §1031 exchange own a single property in a single market with perhaps a single tenant, operated either by themselves or a small local property manager. That is a very concentrated egg-to-basket ratio.

Sponsored real estate investment programs offer the opportunity to own a fractional interest in:

- Tens or hundreds of millions of dollars of real estate
- Assets that were sourced and operated by an institutional real estate firm
- Properties managed by a regional or national property-management company with hundreds or even thousands of employees
- Programs that have been subjected to multiple layers of due diligence, with an offering memorandum that includes a professional business plan and detailed financial projections
- A diversified rent roll that, in the case of multifamily, senior

housing or self-storage portfolios, could include several hundred tenants

- Potentially an array of properties across multiple offerings that could include numerous asset types across various cities or states

Does all of this mean that the opportunity to own a passive program is "better" than your current property? Only you can be the judge of that, after analyzing and comparing both your rental and specific offerings.

3. POSSIBLY GENERATE HIGHER INCOME

In Chapter IIIA, we set forth a tool to estimate your current Equity Yield Rate. It is important that you have at least a ballpark figure for your rental property.

At the time of publication, the first-year cash-on-cash distribution rate for securitized §1031 programs averages approximately 5% (this metric is the equivalent of your Equity Yield Rate). There is no guarantee that this rate will be maintained or that the property will produce distributions at all. Nevertheless, assuming that the property can sustain this rate over the life of the program, it is possible that the typical offering will produce a higher yield than your current rental.

Fluctuations in distributions, if they occur, typically are the result of material unanticipated changes in expenses. Most offering memorandums include a detailed 10-year projection of revenues, expenses and distributions. You may find that the anticipated income potential is attractive, especially compared to your current property. And in many instances, the depreciable property in a passive program may be greater than your own, resulting in less taxable income.

4. ...ALL WHILE DEFERRING OR AVOIDING CAPITAL-GAINS TAXES

It is possible to improve your life, your real estate and your income potential...and defer your capital-gains taxes all at the same time.

If you invest in a qualified exchange program, when that property is sold you retain the same options you have today: 1) take the proceeds and pay the taxes, or 2) return to owning traditional real estate, or 3) invest in another passive program.

By conducting successive §1031 exchanges, you can avoid paying capital-gains taxes altogether, preserving the full value of your real estate for your heirs.

Passive real estate programs do have higher fees, often higher leverage, and are less liquid than other real estate investments. You will have far less control than directly-owned and -operated property. The possible trade-off is a hassle-free investment in institutional-caliber real estate with a potentially higher income.

The journey of a career-long real estate investor can be truly wonderful. As landlords, you provide a fundamental service to your fellow humans: a shelter for someone's home or business. You develop and employ skills in a variety of areas, including real estate but also finance, marketing, construction, management, accounting, law and countless other areas of business. It seems there is always more to learn and more to do. While the risks you take in real estate investing have been significant, we know the rewards—both personal and financial—are usually well worth it.

Some of you will choose to manage your real estate holdings for as long as you can get out of bed in the morning. Others may decide at some point to "cash in your chips" and retire from the business to pursue other interests in life. It is our sincere hope that, no matter where you are in your real estate journey, you have picked up something new from this book, or at least were reminded of something in your memory bank that was helpful to you.

We wrote this guide in response to one over-arching observation. Far too many real estate investors have passed the point where the business of real estate is fun and rewarding. Yet many landlords lack all of the knowledge necessary to retire from the business gracefully and without a heavy tax burden. If we have accomplished our goal with this book, we provided some new perspectives and strategies that opened your eyes to an exciting new possibility.

In other words, you really can retire from being a landlord.

Sources

---

[1] https://www.mysmartmove.com/SmartMove/blog/6-rental-statistics-landlords-need-know.page

[2] https://www.mysmartmove.com/SmartMove/blog/26-rental-stats-landlords-need-know-infographic.page

[3] *Ibid*

[4] http://www.fastevictionservice.com/blog/how-long-does-it-take-to-evict-a-tenant-in-california/

[5] https://expressevictions.com

[6] Oregon Senate Bill 608, 2019: https://legiscan.com/OR/text/SB608/2019

[7] https://www.freedoniagroup.com/industry-study/building-maintenance-services-3002.htm

[8] https://www.hud.gov/program_offices/fair_housing_equal_opp/fair_housing_rights_and_obligations

[9] 42 U.S. Code § 3612

[10] https://www.federalregister.gov/documents/2018/07/16/2018-15116/adjustment-of-civil-monetary-penalty-amounts-for-2018

[11] https://www.avail.co/education/guides/fair-housing-laws/penalties-for-fair-housing-violations

[12] https://realestate.findlaw.com/owning-a-home/homeowner-liability-invitees-licensees-and-trespassers.html

[13] https://www.gspalaw.com/the-law-of-premises-liability-an-overview/

[14] https://www.mcgeorge.edu/documents/Publications/_06_Steiner_MasterMLR39.pdf, p. 177

[15] https://cleanfax.com/market-research/2018-restoration-benchmarking-survey-report/

[16] http://superrestoration.com/2018-trends-to-watch-in-the-restoration-industry/

[17] http://www.wshblaw.com/2017-mold-litigation-update-big-dollars-questionable-claims-reflect-continuing-trends/

[18] https://www.adr.org/sites/default/files/Consumer_Rules_Web_0.pdf

[19] https://www.congress.gov/116/bills/s610/BILLS-116s610is.xml

[20] https://caselaw.findlaw.com/ca-court-of-appeal/1895003.html

[21] https://money.cnn.com/interactive/pf/real estate/natural-disaster-risk-map/index.html?iid=EL

[22] The CoStar indices are constructed using a repeat sales methodology,

widely considered the most accurate measure of price changes for real estate. This methodology measures the movement in the prices of commercial properties by collecting data on actual transaction prices. When a property is sold more than once, a sales pair is created. The prices from the first and second sales are then used to calculate price movement for the property. The aggregated price changes from all of the sales pairs are used to create a price index.
https://www.costargroup.com/docs/librariesprovider3/pr---ccrsi-files/ccrsi-release---sep2019.xlsx?sfvrsn=439e08a4_2

[23] U.S. Constitution Amend. XVI

[24] *Brushaber v. Union Pacific Railroad Co.*, 240 U.S. 1, at 20 (1916)

[25] https://files.taxfoundation.org/20190419110809/An-Overview-of-Capital-Gains-Taxes1.pdf

[26] *Ibid*

[27] https://www.irs.gov/publications/p946#en_US_2018_publink1000107317

[28] https://www.irs.gov/pub/irs-pdf/p946.pdf

[29] https://taxfoundation.org/publications/state-business-tax-climate-index/

[30] *Eisner v. McComber*, 252 U.S. 189, 207 (1919)

[31] Borden, Bradley T. Tax-Free Like-Kind Exchanges. Kingston: Civic Research Institute, 2015, at 1.2[3]

[32] H.R. Rep. No. 73-704, at 13 (1934), from Borden, supra

[33] Borden, supra, at 1.2[3]

[34] *Starker v. United States*, 602 F.2d 1341 (9th Cir. 1979)

[35] Treas. Reg. § 1.1031(k)

[36] https://www.irs.gov/publications/p537#en_US_2018_publink1000221670

[37] CA FTB Notice 2019-05

[38] IRS Revenue Procedure 2008-16

[39] IRS FS-2008-18

[40] Joint Committee on Taxation, 115th Congress, 2d Session, *General Explanation of Public Law 115-97.* Washington: U.S. Government Publishing Office, 2018

[41] https://www.irs.gov/businesses/cost-segregation-audit-techniques-guide-chapter-1-introduction#3

[42] *Whiteco Industries, Inc. v. Commissioner,* 65 T.C. 664 (1975)

[43] https://www.mlrpc.com/articles/understanding-qualified-improvement-property-depreciation-changes/

[44] https://www.irs.gov/publications/p537#en_US_2018_publink100043409

[45] CA FTB Notice 2019-05

[46] *Maloney v. Commissioner,* 93 T.C. 89 (1989)

[47] Joint Committee on Taxation, 107th Congress, 1st Session, *Study of the Overall State of the Federal Tax System and Recommendations for Simplification, Pursuant to Section 8022(3)(B) Of The Internal Revenue Code Of 1986,* Washington: U.S. Government Publishing Office, 2001, Vol. III, from Borden, supra, at 7.3[2]

[48] Instructions for Form 1065, https://www.irs.gov/instructions/i1065#idm140538035818256, Questions 11 and 12

[49] *In the Matter of Consolidated Appeals of Rago Development Corp., et al,* Cal. Board of Equalization, June 23, 2015

[50] PLRs 200709036, 200712013,200728008, 201027036, from Investment Property Exchange Services, Inc. ("IPX"), *1031 Exchange Topics.* 2019. www.ipx1031.com.

[51] Borden, supra, at 3.6[4][a]

[52] Internal Revenue Code §§267(b)(2), 267(c)(4), 707(b)(1), from Borden, supra

[53] https://www.irsvideos.gov/Individual/education/FIRPTA

[54] IRS Revenue Procedure 2000-37

[55] IPX, supra

[56] *Estate of George H. Bartell v. Commissioner,* 147 T.C. 5 (2016)

[57] https://www.treasury.gov/press-center/press-releases/Documents/rr0486.pdf

[58] *Ibid*

[59] Mountain Dell Consulting, LLC

[60] https://www.irs.gov/pub/irs-drop/rp-02-22.pdf

[61] *SEC v. W.J. Howey Co.,* 328 U.S. 293, 90 L.Ed. 1244, 66 S.Ct. 1100 (1946)

[62] https://www.census.gov/newsroom/press-releases/2019/subcounty-population-estimates.html

[63] https://www.bls.gov/web/metro/laummtrk.htm

[64] https://www.usatoday.com/story/money/2019/07/30/jobs-these-cities-adding-most-jobs-employment-growth/39806157/

[65] https://www.apartmentlist.com/rentonomics/top-10-large-cities-with-the-biggest-rent-growth-within-last-year/

[66] Linneman Associates, *The Linneman Letter,* Volume 14, Issue 2, Summer 2014

[67] *Ibid*

This page intentionally left blank

About the Authors

Richard D. Gann

Richard D. Gann practiced law for nine years in the fields of real estate taxation and estate planning, helping clients reduce taxes on their properties and investments, before transitioning into financial services in 2006. His inspiration for helping property owners was his grandfather, Paul Gann, author of California's Proposition 13. Richard developed and supervised a retail securities division of Grubb & Ellis, offering passive exchange programs.

At Steadfast Companies, he helped lead a capital-markets team that raised over $1.5 billion to acquire and revitalize over 100 apartment communities across the country. He also helped create a §1031-exchange program there, designed for investors seeking to co-invest in REIT-owned properties. Richard then joined 1031 Capital Solutions as a Managing Partner. He attended UCLA and California Western School of Law, and today lives in Portland, Oregon.

Jason L. McMurtry

Jason L. McMurtry is the founder and managing partner of 1031 Capital Solutions, a company that specializes in helping real estate investors retire from real estate using passive exchange programs. Jason began his career in financial services in 1997 and has helped transact more than half a billion dollars in §1031 exchange securities transactions. He has presented hundreds of seminars and courses throughout the country on the subjects of §1031 exchanges, DSTs and other real estate and securities investments.

Jason holds multiple securities registrations with FINRA and is an Investment Advisor Representative. He also holds a California real estate license. Jason graduated in 1996 from the University of California Santa Barbara with a degree in Philosophy and earned his MBA from South University. He lives in San Diego County, California.

Made in USA - Kendallville, IN
1205218_9780578630854
01.06.2021 1245